To

_____

From

_____

Date

_____

STORIES TO WARM A Mother's HEART

True Stories of Hope and Inspiration

EDITED BY JILL JONES

Guideposts

Stories to Warm a Mother's Heart

ISBN-10: 0824945263
ISBN-13: 978-0-8249-4526-8

Published by Guideposts
16 East 34th Street
New York, New York 10016
Guideposts.org

Distributed by Ideals Publications, a Guideposts company
2630 Elm Hill Pike, Suite 100
Nashville, Tennessee 37214

Guideposts and *Ideals* are registered trademarks of Guideposts.

Acknowledgments
Every attempt has been made to credit the sources of copyrighted material used in this book. If any such acknowledgment has been inadvertently omitted or miscredited, receipt of such information would be appreciated.

Scripture references are from the following sources: The Holy Bible, King James Version (KJV). The Holy Bible, New International Version®, NIV® Copyright © 1973, 1978, 1984, 2011 by Biblica, Inc.™ Used by permission of Zondervan. All rights reserved worldwide. The Holy Bible, English Standard Version® (ESV), copyright © 2001 by Crossway Bibles, a publishing ministry of Good News Publishers. Used by permission.

Cover and interior design by Thinkpen Design, Inc. | www.thinkpendesign.com

Printed and bound in China

10 9 8 7 6 5 4 3 2 1

Contents

Introduction 1

Five for Five *by Shawnelle Eliasen* 3

Mama and the Piggy Bank *by Lucille Campbell* 10

Ange's Boy *by Marilyn Helleberg* 13

Mama Knew Best *by Rocco DiSpirito* 18

Getting the Message *by Pat Egan Dexter* 24

Words to Grow On *by Dee Wallace Stone* 27

"Take Me Home" *by Karen Kingsbury* 29

You've Got Cake *by Richard Hagerman* 36

The Sureness Within *by Mona Kent* 39

Family First *by Niki Taylor* .44

The Day Norman Rockwell Painted Mother

    by Virginia Morton 51

Little Smidgeons *by Pauline Jensen* 56

Mother's Strength *by Maria Massei-Rosato* 60

Lauren's Dream *by Laura Wray* 69

My Mom's Best Recipes *by Andra Olenik* 75

Come Live with Us *by Dorothy DeBolt* 79

That's My Mom! *by Arthur A. Guenther* 86

"Lord, Keep My Kids Safe" *by Mae Bertha Carter* 91

"Hello, Mother? I'm in Trouble!" *by Beverly Heirich* 98

No Mere Coincidence *by Pamela Freeman* 106

Mama Chavez's Cocina *by Harriette Chavez* 109

Mom, Interrupted *by Sheryl Smith-Rodgers* 114

Marine Moms *by Amber Howe* 120

Hockey Mom *by Becky Rochford* 122

To the Lighthouse *by Jenn Gentlesk* 128

A Test of Love *by Shar Boerema* 133

Homeless Babies and Babyless Homes *by Mary Pickford* 138

The Mother I Had Always Known *by Barbara Wernecke Durkin* 144

Never Far Away *by Carol L. Mackay* 149

The Perfect Card *by Mavis Chaplin* 151

A Song for Mom *by Edward Grinnan* 157

"Please Save My Babies" *by Monica Soto* 159

Spring Break? *by Dawn Meehan* 166

Little Camper on the Prairie *by Sue Catron* 172

One Look of Love *by Deena Clark Farris* 179

Introduction

A mother's love is a gift to be celebrated every day. Whether mothers are affectionate or stern, biological or adoptive, fun-loving or all business, that spirit of love shines through in the way they take care of us, guide us, and support us.

In these true stories, real mothers share their vulnerabilities, their challenges, and those moments of wonder that make them thank God for giving them children. These are women who do their best to bless their children every day in big and small ways. Like the mom who shares a day with her daughter at the lighthouse of her childhood or the mother who helps her eighteen-year-old handicapped son adapt to his new home.

They may be full-time mothers, busy career women, church volunteers, responsible daughters, loving wives, or several of those things at once. But the mothers in these stories offer inspiration and heartwarming encouragement for other moms. Their stories celebrate all the facets of motherhood: the joys, the faith, the determination that make mothers such a blessing from God.

Five for Five

BY SHAWNELLE ELIASEN

I'd always wanted a daughter. I come from a family of girls. Each of my three sisters has a girl. Naturally, I thought I was meant to have a little girl of my own.

My husband Lonny and I had our first child, a beautiful baby boy. I figured our girl would come along later. Our second child was a son too. So was our third. And our fourth.

My fifth pregnancy wasn't a surprise. Lonny and I planned for a big family. But we did consider the likelihood that this baby would be our last. I loved my boys utterly. It was just time to have that girl I'd dreamed of.

I pushed back the first ultrasound to early January so the baby would be developed enough to identify gender. Being pregnant at almost forty warranted the super ultrasound at the university medical school. I lay on an exam table, Lonny standing beside me, as the doctor moved the transducer over my belly. The baby was healthy and strong. Only one question remained.

I closed my eyes and pictured my little girl. Wisps of blond hair escaped her ponytail. Her eyes were wide and green. She wore cotton and crochet on top, and bare pink toes fringed out from frayed jeans. Her gentle spirit was evident in the way she moved. She was mine to teach, mine to mold, mine to pour myself into.

A fresh squirt of goop on my belly jarred me back to reality. "Are you ready to know what you've got?" asked the doctor. Lonny drew my hand into his, and I nodded. Our eyes were fixed on the monitor. The marbled image on the screen moved closer.

I was pregnant with our fifth son.

Everything about the walk through the university parking lot was slow. Conversation was slow. Our pace was slow. Even the snowflakes that shook from the clouds were slow. "You know, Shawnelle, you are an awesome mom to our boys," Lonny said. "No one could do better."

"I adore our boys," I said.

"They'll be great men," he said, "because of you."

That I wasn't so sure about. I was gentle, sensitive by nature. I loved books, not bugs and baseball. I worried that my boys would need more than I could give them, especially as they got older.

"Are you okay?" Lonny asked.

"Sure," I said. But I wasn't, and I was ashamed of it. We had lost a baby early in our marriage. We'd struggled through a time of infertility. I had friends who couldn't conceive. I understood the fragile blessing of a baby. I just couldn't control the tears.

That night I waited for Lonny's breathing to fall into the even rhythm of sleep before I crept from our bed. I stepped around the action figures and dinosaurs in the hall and curled up in our wing chair in the family room.

God, are You sure You've got this right? I asked. *I'm confident I can raise a daughter well. I have so much to teach her. But I'm not sure how to raise strong men. I just don't feel qualified.* I strained to hear a reply. Nothing except the *tick-tock* of our grandfather clock.

Winter—and my pregnancy—progressed. March brought a thick end-of-season snow that sogged through our mittens as my boys and I played at our friend Sue's farm. Sue was the ultimate boy's mom. An all-star. I admired and envied her. I'd seen her wrestle her son to the ground and hold him for a ten count. She could send a football soaring and wallop a baseball to next Tuesday. And she could nail a moving target with a March-heavy snow bomb.

"Over here, Mom," my firstborn, Logan, called. He popped up from behind a snow bank.

Grant, my second son, bounded up. "Snow dogs unleashed!" Samuel and Gabriel, my two youngest, charged. All my boys were armed with snowballs. All fired at me. Slush snaked past my collar and down my back. I wanted to call it quits then and there. If I had my way, we'd be snuggled under warm blankets, drinking hot chocolate and reading aloud from a great book.

Instead, my boys waited for payback. I knew they wanted to be chased down and attacked. I scooped up snow. I jogged toward my herd of boys. I aimed and fired. And I missed every single one. My belly, thick with baby, and my lack of natural athletic ability prevented proper retaliation.

Sue sprinted toward us, chasing her son. Her long stride narrowed the distance. She tackled him, pinned him, and bounced back up. Then she ripped after my boys. She scooped and fired like a combat machine. One, two, three! Snow missiles exploded on bright parkas. Only Gabriel, my toddler, was spared. He squealed with delight anyway. My boys peeled after Sue. I stood in the falling snow and watched, longing to be a fun mom for my boys, a wrestling mom. To be good at what they liked to do.

Spring came. Lonny and I took long walks along the Mississippi. One afternoon when the river was flat and smooth and the air heavy with rain, we walked hand in hand. Our two youngest ran ahead, filling their pockets with rocks, poking at anything they could with sticks. "It won't be long now," Lonny said. We both looked at my swaying belly. "Are you settled with this, Shawnelle? Having another son?"

"I love this baby entirely," I said. "Sight unseen. But I do still wonder."

"About what?" Lonny asked.

"I wonder what God is doing. I want to be the best mom I can be. I just don't know how to put what I'm good at into boys." Lonny was silent. "And I want to be what they need me to be. I want to teach them what they need to know. I want to be on the same page with them. Sometimes I feel like I'm not even in the same book."

"You are exactly the mom our boys need, Shawnelle. One hundred percent. Why else would God keep giving you men to raise with me?"

Our conversation halted. Ahead lay a little boy's dream. A puddle the size of a wading pool. Before I could stop them, Samuel and Gabriel peeled off their shoes and socks and leapt gleefully into the muddy water. I sighed. Puddle stomping. Another thing that would never come naturally to me.

Our baby's arrival drew closer. We decided to name him Isaiah. I was waking up a lot at night. Often I'd make my way to the family room, curl in our wing chair, and take my questions to God. *You made me quiet and gentle. You gave me the ability to be sensitive to others and care for their needs. How do I fold these things into my boys? I want to raise strong men.*

At last it was time for Isaiah to join our family. That morning broke calm and clear. Because I was a repeat customer, my obstetrician let me choose where I wanted to be on the surgical line-up. I was scheduled to be the first C-section of the day.

Lonny and I loaded our sons into the Suburban and drove to the hospital. I went into the surgical prep room alone. Once I was fully decorated with tubes and monitors, the nurses stepped out and shut the door.

It creaked open again. One by one, my boys shuffled in. They assembled alongside my bedrails. Lonny stood near the headboard. "You'll be okay, Mom. I know you will. We've prayed for you," Grant said. His eyes were brimming.

"Thank you for doing this, Mom," Logan said, his voice quivering. "Are you comfortable? Can I get you another blanket?"

"I have your slippers ready. For when you're done. I love you, Mom," Samuel said. His lower lip trembled.

"Love you, Mama," echoed Gabriel. "Love you."

My four strong boys. Two to my right. Two to my left. Eight hands rested on the white sheet that covered me. Some of the hands were nearly man-sized. Some were still small and could barely reach me. Their gazes, though, were what drew me. My eyes locked on the wide green eyes of each of my sons. And what I saw there stirred my soul. Compassion. Mercy. Gentleness. Love. These qualities, the ones that God had given me, were not lost. They were not bound by gender. And they did not flow into my sons as a weakness. These qualities helped make a man, just as Lonny told me—a man strong enough to care for others.

I am a wrestling mom, I thought. I wrestled with God over His plan for our family, and He showed me how He'd let me win. With Logan. Grant. Samuel. Gabriel. And now, Isaiah. I couldn't wait to hold my fifth son in my arms and look into his wide green eyes.

Divine Proof

*How wise should we be if, with joyful certainty,
we accepted each unfolding of His will as a proof
of His faithfulness and love!*

SUSANNAH SPURGEON

Mama and the Piggy Bank

BY LUCILLE CAMPBELL

It was at a family gathering on the evening her last child graduated that Mother confided to us the big dream of her life. She, who had never been one hundred miles from home, wanted to journey halfway around the world to Jerusalem.

"Just think, I could see where Jesus was born in Bethlehem." Her eyes were bright with her dream. "Maybe I could walk where Jesus walked."

Mother had never had a real vacation. Widowed and with young children, she had to work hard to support us—washing and ironing. Later as supervisor of the linen room in a large hospital, Mother had used her vacation time for family emergencies like the two-week period when four of us children had whooping cough. Another vacation was spent beside a hospital bed after one of my brothers had been hurt in an auto accident.

After we children learned of Mother's dream, we called a special family get-together. We would give Mother the grand vacation she always wanted. An immense china piggy bank was placed in the center of her living room table. Into the bank went all the cash that all of us could spare.

But Mother, so penny-pinching for herself, spent lavishly for others. The pig, getting so fat one day, might find himself very lean the next. Mother was always robbing him. One time she decided that a little girl's life was being ruined by her extremely misshapen nose. Mother helped pay to have the nose reshaped through plastic surgery. Then there was the very intelligent boy who just had to go to college. Mother gave him financial assistance. An old friend had a stroke—Mother felt that a therapist and special equipment would help her friend recover, so Mother helped with the expenses. At the start of each year Mother would say, "Now this is the year for my trip to Jerusalem." But then it seemed that a new grandchild began arriving every year and Mother took her vacation time to be on hand to help the burdened mother.

Then one day Mother collapsed at work. When we took her home a few days later, the doctor told us that her heart was badly damaged and she must rest a great deal.

Back at home that first day, we had to dissuade Mother from getting our supper. We settled her on the porch to watch the children play on the lawn. From the living room where I sat with my brother I could see her. She looked so old and frail. My brother opened the piggy bank. She had robbed it again.

Only two crumpled bills, a few nickels, and a cascade of pennies tumbled out. "It doesn't matter about the money," I sobbed. "She can never take her vacation now, never walk where Jesus walked. Never, now." My brother thrust his handkerchief into my hand. "Here, stop crying," he ordered gruffly, but there were tears in his eyes too. "You know very well she's been walking where Jesus walked every day of her life," he said. And she had. She walked, serving, as He had walked. Why should I cry for such a successful, victorious life? Comforted, I dried my eyes.

Light of Life

I looked to Jesus, and I found
In Him my Star, my Sun:
And in that light of life I'll walk,
'Til traveling days are done!

HORATIUS BONAR

Ange's Boy

BY MARILYN HELLEBERG

I f Tom had been a few years younger the night he came to us, shivering from the January cold and clinging to his black dog, I could have put my arms around him and said, "Go ahead and cry, honey. Let it all out." It would have been easier that way. But instead he was fourteen and dry-eyed, and his grief was tightly locked up somewhere inside of him; so I petted the dog he held so close and led them both into the warm kitchen.

The mother in me grieved for the part of him that was still a child as I watched my husband Rex carry in the few belongings that were all Tom had left of his mother and father. The Christmas-night car accident that had taken the lives of Tom's parents had also left a big hole in my husband's life. Tom's mother was Rex's oldest sister—the one who had taken over the family when their own mother had died. Now it was our turn to take care of Ange's boy.

I had been so sure that this was the right decision, but as I showed Tom the curtained-off room I had fixed for him and went back into the kitchen to make popcorn for the family, the awesome responsibility I had assumed suddenly began to close in on me. I opened the kitchen window a little, even though it was snowing outside. Our small house was already crowded with our own family of five plus two dogs, and our eight-month-old baby demanded so much of my time. How would I ever work one more person into my crowded household and busy schedule? More important still, how could I ever reach the brutally wounded spirit of this quiet, shy teen-ager who would be embarrassed by any physical expression of our love?

The children were all clamoring for Tom's attention now, as we sat at the kitchen table eating our popcorn. I think he was glad when I said it was time for all to get to bed. I hoped that Tom wouldn't notice the tension in my voice as I said good night to him.

I noticed first that there was more washing, more ironing, more mess because we were so crowded. And I was spending more time doing the never finished things—grocery shopping, cooking, dishes, chauffeuring.

Tom, meanwhile, was facing his devastating loss with courage and manliness. Though he was a guest for the first two weeks, in an atmosphere of strained politeness and overconcern, it wasn't long before he was "flying" the baby around the house and laughing and joking and, yes, fighting with the older children. He seemed to adjust quickly to the new school.

But I knew that there were times when the sealed wound ached within him. When we made a trip to Lincoln and stopped to check the empty house, when one of our children brought out an old family picture in which Ange was holding Tom on her lap, when he was elected to the student council at school and someone said, "Your mother would have been so proud of you." At these times especially I wanted so desperately to put my arms around Ange's boy and say, "I understand how you feel."

But somehow I just couldn't. There seemed to be an impenetrable wall surrounding his hurt; and though I sensed that the boy on the other side of the wall was trying to get through it, too, we simply could not reach each other.

In spite of worries and added work, we managed to get through the winter and almost before I realized it, spring was here. I was not surprised that Tom seemed depressed and edgy after the trip to visit his parents' graves on Memorial Day. The next day was gray and gloomy and the children had been bickering all day. So I didn't think much about it when Tom stomped out the door with his dog on a leash after a fight with our ten-year-old over nothing at all. But our daughter followed him and in twenty minutes she was back, breathless and on the verge of tears. "Mom! Tom's running away. He's on the fairgrounds road."

I put down the potato I was peeling, phoned my husband, and left the older children to watch the baby. I drove to and through the fairgrounds, then circled block after block, but Tom had disappeared. Tears started burning my eyes. *O God, please bring him home.*

By this time, Rex was also searching in his car, so I started home to check on the children. Tears were stinging my cheeks now as I realized how much I loved this tall, quiet boy. Not because I felt sorry for him. Not because I was expected to love him. Not even because he was Ange's boy. I loved him because he was Tom and because somewhere deep inside of me, there was a place especially for him—a place no one else could ever fill if I lost him now.

Then all at once I was aware of something strong and solid that had been running all the way through the kinks and tangles of adjustment—something that had helped me cope with the added responsibility—that had made the locked doors a challenge instead of a defeat—that was making our busy lives rich and full instead of merely crowded. It was a feeling—warm and buoyant—like the feeling you have when your child tracks mud across your newly scrubbed floor to give you a big hug and kiss, and incongruously, you feel suddenly happy, realizing how lucky you are to have people needing your love. The extra work and responsibility then become a blessing because there is love.

As I pulled into the driveway, the children came running out to meet me. Tom had come back while we were out searching.

I found him lying on his bed, scratching his dog's ears. As I sat on the edge of the bed with one hand on his shoulder and the other petting his dog, I heard myself say, "I understand how you feel, Tom."

The wall had crumbled and I had at last entered the place where his grief was. Then Ange's boy said, "I'm glad to be home."

And I realized, with a sudden stab of joy, that he meant right here, in our house.

The Mother Instinct

There is an instinct in a woman to love most her own child—and an instinct to make any child who needs her love, her own.

ROBERT BRAULT

Mama Knew Best

It's a question I'm asked often: "Why did you become a chef?" People who've seen me on TV figure I do it to be famous. Or they hear about my new cookbook and think I'm in it for the money. For me, cooking has never been about those things. My desire to be a chef goes back to something I learned from a great cook many years ago, in the small kitchen of a two-story red-and-white house on Ninetieth Avenue in Jamaica, Queens, a rough, working-class neighborhood of New York City.

Mama's kitchen. It was a long ways from where she grew up, the small Italian village of San Nicola Baronia. There, her family prepared their meals in a pot hung over a fire pit. Mama's mother, my nonna, worked with what she had, which wasn't much. Yet Nonna would always make something delicious and nourishing. When Mama came here to the States at twenty-four, she brought those culinary skills with her.

My earliest memory of watching her in the kitchen is from when I was about six. My brother and sister were much older and out hanging with their friends; my father worked all day as a carpenter, so Mama was home alone with me. She was making her frittata, a kind of dense Italian omelet. I reached up to the counter to grab a piece, still warm from the stove. I couldn't help myself; the delicious aromas of gooey parmesan cheese, sautéed onions and peppers and eggs wafted through the air. "No, no, Rocco," Mama scolded me. "Don't you touch; this is for the Rosary Society."

That was another thing Mama brought with her from the old country—her faith. For her, cooking wasn't only about filling stomachs. "Food is love," she always told me, and Mama shared her food, and love, with others in our neighborhood. The Rosary Society wasn't exactly the place a restless kid like me wanted to be, but where Mama and her food went, I went.

The smell of the frittata kept escaping the covered pan as Mama carried it to church. By the time we arrived, I was ravenous. And I wasn't the only one. "Nicolina, did you bring your frittata?" one of the ladies asked.

"Of course," Mama responded. But before we could eat, we had to pray. Everyone stood together and bowed their heads, reciting the prayer. It seemed to last forever. But Mama's food was worth the wait. "This is just like the frittata my mother used to make," one woman exclaimed. "I need the recipe," said another. Seeing the women smile and thank my mother showed me for the first time the power of food to bring people together. Prayer nourished the soul, food nourished your body and, when prepared with a lot of love, both could make strangers into family.

I began to spend more time in Mama's kitchen. My first "dish" was a simple one. Mama handed me a little rolled-out piece of dough and showed me how to fry it up in a skillet. When it was golden brown, we'd drizzle some honey on it and top it off with a sprinkle of sugar. Pizza fritta, she called it. She'd make them into shapes like her mama used to do. Those little pieces of crispy dough seemed so easy to make. Until I tried to make them by myself one day and set the hot pan down on the wooden counter. My heart sank when I picked the pan back up to find a large black circle burned into the surface beneath it. "What have you done?" Mama scolded when she saw the damage. But she forgave me. She was grateful I'd found something that held my interest, because, in our neighborhood, there were a lot of distractions.

Few kids in our neighborhood went to college or got good jobs. A lot of them sought out cheap thrills and easy scores. More than once, I got shaken down for money by drug addicts and dealers on my walk back from school. Mama wouldn't let me fall into the quicksand that claimed so many kids. When I was eleven, there was a record I really wanted to buy, so I asked for a raise in my allowance. Mama looked at me like I was crazy. "You need to get a job," she told me. "You must work for what you want."

Mama knew a thing or two about that. The very day she came off the boat from Italy, she went straight to work at an uncle's tailor shop and worked for the next nine hours. For three years she was a seamstress. After marrying my father, she took a part-time job knitting sweaters—getting seventy-five cents for every dozen she made. Yet she saved enough money to help bring our whole extended family to America.

So I got work at a pizzeria—thirty dollars a week sweating in front of a hot oven, covered in sauce and grease. I loved it. Here was my chance to do what Mama did, make people happy with my food—even if it was just pizza.

We moved to Long Island a few years later, and Mama got a job as a school lunch lady—appropriate, I thought, for a woman who loved cooking for her kids. I moved on from making pizza. At fifteen, I went to work for the New Hyde Park Inn, an award-winning restaurant, and I started to think seriously about culinary school. Mama had never gone to college and still couldn't speak English that well, but she encouraged me.

At nineteen, after graduating culinary school, I traveled to Paris. I struggled for a while, working at a burger joint and sleeping at a friend's place, but eventually I landed my dream job working under a Michelin-starred chef. Success there led me back to New York, where I became head chef at a restaurant called Union Pacific and started getting great reviews. Then NBC offered me a reality show that would chronicle the creation of my own restaurant, Rocco's.

I knew my restaurant had to be a place that served my family's food. Who better to help me than my own family? I hired my uncle to make the wine and the sausages, my aunt to make the fresh pasta. There was never any doubt that Mama would be involved. She was retired when I made her the offer to be Rocco's meatball maker. I worried it might be too much for her at seventy-seven.

Mama became the star of The Restaurant, both in the kitchen and on TV. Fans stopped her in the street and asked her for autographs. It was like that scene I'd witnessed as a little kid at the Rosary Society—people finding joy in Mama's cooking. It may have been my name on the sign, but Mama was the place's heart and soul. When the restaurant closed, I think Mama was more disappointed than I was. "Aren't you happy to be able to retire?" I asked her.

She just shook her head. "At my age, I'm happy to be able to get up in the morning and do something for people."

When Mama turned eighty-three, I realized she was still my greatest teacher. She was given a great talent, one that she passed along to me. She also passed along the important duty that comes with any of God's gifts to us—to share them. It's why she cooked that frittata for her Rosary group. Why she worked as a lunch lady. Why she even gave away her secret meatball recipe in one of my cookbooks. It's why I became a chef. I'm just following her lead.

A Mother's Blessing

My mother was the making of me. She was so true and so sure of me, I felt that I had someone to live for—someone I must not disappoint. The memory of my mother will always be a blessing to me.

THOMAS EDISON

Getting the Message

BY PAT EGAN DEXTER

*I*t's a good thing we've got a pastor who's willing to put up with restless kids, I thought, as I eyed the pair in front of me. I remembered that the pastor had even admitted to having been one of the unruly ones himself.

The present unruliness was making it difficult for my husband and me to concentrate on the church service. The culprits were two young brothers in the pew ahead of us. Their mother sat between them, her attention divided between the altar and her sons. One boy played with a piece of string, winding and rewinding it around his hand; the other cleaned his nails. When they weren't occupied with these diversions, they made faces at each other or exchanged pokes. Every little while the mother touched one son or the other in warning.

I knew this young woman only slightly, a single mom trying to raise two sons alone. Every Sunday she was in church with the boys. They were too old for the nursery and too young to be left home alone. But obviously they were too poorly behaved to bring to church.

What a waste of her time to bring them here, I thought. *I'm sure none of the three hears anything that's said.*

As I watched, the smaller boy reached behind his mother's back and tweaked his brother's sleeve. I felt like moving to another pew. But, even more, I felt sorry for the woman. And I didn't want to add to the embarrassment I assumed she must feel.

At that point in the service, the priest asked all the mothers in the congregation to rise. The young mother in front of us stood up. The priest spent a few minutes lauding the job of motherhood. Then he asked all those seated who agreed with him to reach out and touch a mother and join him in prayer and thanks for all mothers.

The two brothers quickly stood and put their arms around their mother. One leaned his head against her shoulder, the other held her hand. They prayed out loud with the rest of the congregation. The mother clasped her sons tightly and stood tall. When she turned her head, I could see her face glowing with pride and happiness.

After the prayer was over we all sat down again. The boys resumed their fidgeting, their mother's attention was still divided. But the situation didn't bother me anymore. I'd seen that this small family understood the essence of what Jesus taught, of what people come to church to learn—and to express: God is love.

The warmth of that love was filling me, conquering my annoyance. I prayed: *Thank You, God, for showing me my own shortsightedness. Now I see how much can be accomplished—despite "unruliness"—in Your house.*

Patient Love

A mother's love is patient and forgiving when all others are forsaking, it never fails or falters, even though the heart is breaking.

HELEN STEINER RICE

Words to Grow On

BY DEE WALLACE STONE

A s an actress I've often played mothers. I was the mother in the film *E.T.*, the mother in *Cujo*, and the mother in the Lassie series on TV. In November 1988, after years of waiting, my husband Chris and I had a baby daughter, Gabrielle. Right from the beginning we decided that we would see to it that Gabrielle was brought up in a positive atmosphere, that whenever we could we would affirm those qualities we hoped she'd take with her into adulthood. We prayed that she'd be happy, healthy, and balanced, with a good sense of self-esteem.

Psychologists have said that the most impressionable time in a child's day is the half hour before bedtime. So with Gabrielle we use this period to read her books together and sing to her. Often we sing a lullaby that a friend wrote for her. And always the last thing we do is sing the prayer my parents used to sing to me—a variation on a familiar bedtime prayer:

> Now I lay me down to sleep,
> Angels guarding over me,
> Like the birdies in the trees,
> Heavenly Father, care for me.

The prayer always ends with requests that God bless Mommy and Daddy and grandparents and playmates, and yes, our dogs too—Spirit and Rugs.

But each night as Gabrielle goes to bed there is one blessing that we hope she will take with her as she drifts off to sleep. We tell her that Mommy loves her and Daddy loves her, but above all we affirm these three simple, most powerful words to grow on: God loves you.

Deep and Wide

I pray that you, being rooted and established in love, may have power...to grasp how wide and long and high and deep is the love of Christ.

EPHESIANS 3:17–18 NIV

"Take Me Home"

BY KAREN KINGSBURY

I brushed the bangs from my forehead and clicked SEND on an e-mail, answering a question from a fan about a character in one of my novels.

A child from Haiti. These words popped into my head like an e-mail popping into my inbox. It had been a really long day: working on my new book in the morning, taking care of family and household stuff in the afternoon, then back to my study to answer fan mail in the evening. I tried to dismiss the thought. But it wouldn't be dismissed.

At that time my husband Don and I already had three children but wanted more. Don had a good job as a high school basketball and football coach. I had published half a dozen novels. By any yardstick we were a blessed family.

But when our youngest, Austin, was only three weeks old, he had undergone major surgery to correct an inherited heart defect. He survived, but the ordeal practically killed me. My doctor said that it was fortunate that neither of our other children had inherited the condition. And Don and I didn't want to take a risk with our next child. We started talking about adoption—tentatively at first, then just about every day. We met with an adoption facilitator to explore our options.

"There are plenty of kids in America who need good homes," she told us. "But if you really want to go where the need is greatest, consider Haiti. It's the poorest country in the Western Hemisphere."

The facilitator mentioned one orphanage in particular— Heart of God Ministries, just outside the Haitian capital of Port-au-Prince. Don and I had agreed to take things slow. The orphanage had a website. But we hadn't yet looked at it.

Now, with the kids in bed, Don up in our bedroom reading and me down here in my study with my writing done for the day, I couldn't resist. I typed in the name of the orphanage and clicked.

Heart of God's homepage popped up. "See our list of adoptable kids," said a banner down at the bottom.

Kelsey, our oldest, was twelve. Tyler was seven. Don and I wanted to fill the gap between him and two-year-old Austin. I narrowed my search down and clicked again.

A boy's face appeared on the screen. A boy with big brown eyes and a gentle, tentative smile. I could almost hear God whispering in my ear, "*Adopt that boy.*"

"Emmanuel Jean's grandmother dropped him off a year ago," said the text. "She believed with all her heart that a loving American family would make him their son."

I ran up to our bedroom and pulled Don away from his book. He followed me into my study and leaned over the screen.

"Are you sure?" he asked. "There are hundreds...."

"I know, I know," I said. "It sounds impulsive. Crazy, even. But I just know God wants that boy to be our son."

Don pointed to another banner that offered a free video.

"I guess we'd better get it," he said.

A package showed up about a week later. We hadn't brought up the idea of adoption with our kids yet. We waited till they were all tucked into bed before slipping in the video.

E.J. appeared. Same big brown eyes. Same sweet smile. And the same unmistakable feeling in my soul: he was meant for us.

The next day Don and I printed out E.J.'s picture, placed it in an empty chair in the living room, and called Kelsey, Tyler, and Austin in.

"How would you guys feel about having a new brother?" I asked the kids.

"He looks really friendly," said Kelsey.

"He's five?" Tyler chimed in. "That's right between me and Austin!"

Don and I felt so encouraged we took another look at our finances. Why not adopt two children at once and save ourselves the time and expense of doing it again later! We got back on the website and found another boy, a close friend of E.J.'s. Like him he had a warm, sweet smile that tugged at my heart. Sean.

We initiated the adoption process. The first package of forms that came in the mail was thicker than our phone book.

With each new form we tackled, the reality of what we were getting into hit Don and me harder.

Lying in bed one night, I felt my confidence—that sureness I'd felt when I first saw E.J.'s face on my screen—faltering. A noisy parade of what-ifs marched through my head. Were we taking on too much? Could we do this? Was the decision to adopt two boys really right?

Our adoption facilitator had made clear that Rule Number One of bringing a new child into a home with other children is to love all of them equally. You have to know that your adopted child is your child, end of story. I had three children I'd raised from birth—children who were as much a part of me as the blood that flowed in my veins. Who was I kidding to think I could let two total strangers into my house and be able to treat them with that same closeness? I hugged my pillow. *God, can I really be the mother You want me to be? To five children?*

Two months after E.J.'s face appeared on my computer screen, I boarded a plane for Port-au-Prince. Don would stay with our kids back in the States.

The orphanage—a low brick building surrounded by a wall topped with razor wire—lay on the outskirts of town. Inside, forty-two kids lived in a 1,400-square-foot space. Pigs rooted in garbage just a few feet from the front door. I knocked.

A woman, the head of the orphanage, greeted me. "It's a special day when a parent comes to adopt a child," she told me. "All of the children are so excited that you've come."

She led me out to a walled-off patio with a single cement bench. The kids followed after us. She called two boys out of the crowd—both so skinny their shoulders barely kept the necks of their shirts up. I recognized them instantly. Sean and E.J. I leaned down to hug them, when all at once another little boy emerged from the crowd.

"Hi, Mommy," this one said. Then, in a gesture so familiar it was as though he had known me forever, he brushed the bangs from my forehead.

Who was this child?

The orphanage director explained. The three boys—Sean, E.J. and this third boy, Joshua—were like brothers. For all intents, they were brothers. "Joshua knows you are Sean and E.J.'s mother now," she said. "That makes you his mother too."

It made no difference to Joshua that I wasn't taking him home. In his mind I was his mother nonetheless. How could that be? Trust. A trust beyond all questioning, all judgment, all logic. A trust that could only come from one place.

E.J. and Sean were allowed to come with me to the guest quarters. Joshua waited with the other kids to say good-bye. Surely the reality would set in, and I dreaded the thought of hurting his feelings. I waited for his tears to come.

"Good-bye, Sean, good-bye, E.J.," he said. Then he turned to me. "Good-bye, Mother!" he said without a hint of doubt.

Doubt. It's something we adults are pretty good at. Sometimes it seems like the longer we live, the better we get at it. But it was a skill six-year-old Joshua had yet to learn. A little Haitian boy with no education, few prospects, and barely enough meat on his bones to keep his clothes on, he nonetheless had room in his heart for faith. Faith that I was his mother. He simply knew. The same way I knew that night when those words popped into my head about adopting a child from Haiti. Who was I to tell him he was wrong?

I called Don that night to report on the day's events. I worried it would sound more like a plot from one of my novels than a real-life scenario.

"Honey, I don't know how to say this exactly, but there aren't two boys here for us, there are three." I told him the whole story. "I just can't bear the thought of leaving Joshua behind."

"Well then don't," said Don. "Two, three...bring those boys home."

Only Sean and E.J. could come back to the States with me on that trip. We had to go through the same complicated legal procedures to adopt Joshua. Six months later he joined our family too.

I won't say there weren't any rough patches, because there were. America—with its grocery stores full of food, its hot and cold running water, and its completely alien ways, was a huge challenge for all three of the boys. But they had a family to love them every step of the way. And that's what counted.

Several years later the challenges haven't gone away. But these days they're the kind that any normal American family faces. For one thing, we've got three kids in their teens now, and I don't need to tell any parent out there that that brings a whole new world of hurdles.

Sometimes my life does sound like the plot from one of my books. But that's not so bad, considering whose plot it is.

God's Creation

A family is a group of individuals who are related to one another by marriage, birth, or adoption— nothing more, nothing else. This is not merely human in origin. It is God's marvelous creation.

DR. JAMES DOBSON

You've Got Cake

BY RICHARD HAGERMAN

Mom raised me on her own since I was fourteen years old, when my dad died. It was the depths of the Great Depression, and Mom worked hard to support our family. Still, she always found a way to accommodate my requests for my favorite dessert: Dream Cake. Crunchy, chewy and sweetened with coconut and caramelized brown sugar, it was perfect with a scoop of vanilla ice cream. No campfire wiener roast, church dinner or birthday party could end without everyone munching on Dream Cake, making jokes, and telling stories. When I left home to start premed school, Mom sent her cakes to me in the mail. But my studies were cut short by World War II. At eighteen I was drafted and became a medic in the 1123rd Combat Engineers.

But Mom's Dream Cakes didn't stop. They arrived during my basic training in Mississippi and when we were stationed in England, awaiting deployment to the battlefront. Our unit landed in France the day after Christmas, 1944. Much of Europe remained in the grip of the Nazis. Getting that familiar package in the mail from my mom always lifted my spirits.

Of course, there were socks, newspapers, sweaters, and a little note from Mom. But the big treat was her Dream Cake, wrapped up carefully in wax paper.

I knew my mother sacrificed her ration stamps just to buy the ingredients for my cakes, and that made it even more meaningful.

It was the perfect cake for wartime—a solid hunk of chewy delight, tough enough to resist the tumbling and battering of overseas army mail. Even when shipments were delayed, the cake would still arrive in my hands as delicious as it was when it came out of the oven. Sometimes mail would get backed up and I'd receive two cakes at once! The double dose of cake made me forget the extra wait.

To me, receiving a Dream Cake ranked second in excitement only to a Bob Hope USO show.

All the guys of the 1123rd were familiar with Mom's dessert. "Hey, Hagerman's got that cake again," somebody would shout, and I'd naturally have to divvy up pieces for everybody. I was never quite sure whether my army buddies really liked me or whether they just hung around for the great cake.

The Dream Cake came in handy while our unit was camped in the little town of Tontelange, Belgium, just twenty kilometers away from what would later be known as The Battle of the Bulge.

We cared for injured soldiers on the ground floor of a Belgian home, a space provided by a woman and her ten-year-old daughter, Gheslaine. The man of the house had been captured by the German army. It was a sad and tense situation for everyone.

Then one day a Dream Cake arrived. I invited little Gheslaine and the other soldiers to a cake party. In the flickering lantern-light, we sat around the kitchen table, talking about good times, telling funny stories, and sharing jokes. It was just like those birthday parties and cookouts we used to have back in the States. Thousands of miles away, across an ocean, in the middle of a war zone, I felt closer to home.

Afterward, Gheslaine asked if she could write a note in my letter home to my mom to thank her for the delicious dessert.

My waistline has grown since my tour in Europe, but every so often I spend time in the kitchen and bake a Dream Cake. The second that sweet coconut scent fills my nose, those great memories of family and friends come flooding back. I remember that lantern-lit Belgium kitchen where soldiers shared mouthfuls of Dream Cake and broken conversation with a little Belgian girl.

Mom couldn't reach me, but her cake could. A little taste of home when I needed it most.

When It's Needed

No one ever outgrows the need for a mother's love.

JANETTE OKE

The Sureness Within

BY MONA KENT

The nurse swept into my room with the brisk efficiency of a vacuum cleaner.

"Good morning," she said crisply. "How do you feel?"

As I opened my mouth to answer, she popped in the thermometer and seized my wrist with a no-nonsense grip.

"Now," she declared when she had taken my pulse, "we'll get you ready for breakfast."

I didn't want breakfast, but the thermometer prevented me from telling her, as did the toothbrush she thrust at me and the washcloth she clapped over my mouth. Five high-speed minutes later, my sheets had been jerked taut as a sail in a nor'easter, my pillows pummeled to plumpness, and she was cranking up the headrest as if it were a balky Model-T.

I was itchy with irritation by the time she went off duty, so peevish and hot and miserable that when the nurse who replaced her came in, I drew myself into a knot and pulled up the sheet.

"I don't want anything," I snapped. "Just leave me alone!"

"I'll stay awhile, just in case," she said and her voice was nice. It didn't jostle me. "My name's Miss Elliott."

Watching her move about the room, quickly but with no sense of hurry, I felt the kinks ease out of me. She brought me orange juice, rubbed my back, and listened while I told her how I hated being sick. The pillows seemed softer after she smoothed them, the bed less antagonistic, and when she let down the headrest, I drifted off into a relaxed, healing sleep.

Now, when you're a writer, you're always trying to figure out the why of things and people. During my convalescence, I puzzled away at it. Why did one nurse set my teeth on edge and the other soothe me like the sound of rain?

It came to me one afternoon as I stared up at the ceiling. Miss Elliott cared. The other didn't seem to care about anything except being the fastest, most efficient nurse on the floor. Her patients were stage props necessary to prove her superiority. On the other hand, Miss Elliott wasn't trying to prove anything. Somewhere, deep within herself, she was sure about Miss Elliott, and this certainly set her free to understand and meet her patients' needs.

That freedom...is that what loving is? I wondered. And the idea was so intriguing, I carried it around for months like a coin in my pocket, looking at it, turning, testing it.

Then one day I was at Juvenile Court when two boys around eleven were brought in. Their mothers had been summoned, and one was in tears. I'll always remember her, head down with shame, her hands coarsened by hard work, twisting a sodden handkerchief.

"I've tried so hard to be a good mother, to bring him up right," she told the judge despairingly. Then, turning to the sullen boy, "Why do you act like this and make me so ashamed before the neighbors?"

Johnny's young face grew more sullen, and he didn't answer.

The other mother said nothing. It almost seemed as if she and the boy were alone, so unconscious was she of everything else. For a long time, the boy, who seemed short for his age, inspected the floor with the toe of his shoe. When he finally shot a sidelong glance at his mother, what he saw in her face made him turn toward her.

"They dared me to take the money!" he burst out.

"They?"

"The gang!"

Again she waited...letting him take his own time.

"They said I was afraid, and I'm not! I'm not!"

She put her hand on his shoulder, and something in the gesture said, louder than any words, she understood how that could hurt. Suddenly, all the boy's defenses went down, and he clung to her, sobbing, "Why aren't I as tall as other kids my age? How come I'm such a peewee?"

His mother had no immediate answer because there was none, but now she knew the real trouble, something could be done.

There it was again, I thought. The mother who cried out in such despair was so concerned with proving she was a good mother, she had no time nor energy left with which to meet the boy's need. The other mother, like Miss Elliott, was somehow sure inside, and this gave her a freedom to sense the boy's hurt and offer help in such a way he could accept it.

Still puzzling all this through, I went to a friend who has devoted her life to helping people understand each other. "How did Miss Elliott and the mother learn that sureness?" I asked her.

"Think of life as a rainbow," she answered, "with each person contributing his own special color, pink, blue, green, cerise, and so on. But the only way to fully appreciate all that magnificence is to be able to step from our own color band into the glow of another person. This is what I call loving...the ability to see another and to accept him for what he is, according to the particular color he sends out."

She took down from among her books a copy of the Bible and turned to Genesis.

"Your Miss Elliott and the mother are sure because they live by this," she said and began to read. " 'So God created man in his own image, in the image of God created he him; male and female created he them" (Genesis 1:27 KJV).

She closed the book slowly, and her face was sad.

"When people become guilty or ashamed of who and what they are, when they deny and reject that special loveliness that is themselves, they are denying and rejecting Him who made them in His image. Without God we're no longer sure, and so we lose our power to love."

"In His own image," the words went with me as I turned toward home. That means everyone, I thought, including me!

Truest Friend

*A mother is the truest friend we have, when
trials heavy and sudden, fall upon us; when
adversity takes the place of prosperity; when
friends who rejoice with us in our sunshine desert
us; when trouble thickens around us, still will she
cling to us, and endeavor by her kind precepts and
counsels to dissipate the clouds of darkness,
and cause peace to return to our hearts.*

WASHINGTON IRVING

Family First

BY NIKI TAYLOR

I don't remember the impact. That part of the car accident is a blank. I was in Atlanta that weekend in late April, up from Fort Lauderdale visiting friends.

Next thing I knew I was crawling from the car. A single thought was in my head: Am I okay? Then, right on top of that, came the thought any mother would have: I need to be okay for my kids.

My six-year-old twins, Hunter and Jake, were down in Florida with their dad, my ex-husband. I'd promised my boys I'd only be gone for three days. I had to be all right. Even a short hospital stay would break that promise. I took a look down at myself. Not a scratch. By now my two friends were out of the vehicle too. They looked a little banged up, but seemed okay as well.

Thank You, God....

Suddenly, my abdomen started hurting—a pain more intense than anything I'd ever felt, like my insides were on fire. I lay down on the grass, tears streaming from my eyes.

That's the last thing I remember. I came to in Atlanta's Grady Memorial Hospital. How long had it been? A day? More? What about Jake and Hunter? What about my promise? I tried to speak but there was something in my throat. A tube. I was breathing through a tube.

In bits and pieces, through the haze of my returning consciousness, the doctors explained what had happened. "Your liver was virtually torn in half," one of the surgeons explained.

"How long have I been here?" I scribbled on a pad by my bedside.

"About a month," the doctor said.

A month? No! May was almost gone. What about my boys? I'd missed Mother's Day. Somehow, that stung more than everything else I was hearing. I scribbled another note on the paper. "When can I see Hunter and Jake?"

"I'm sorry, Niki. The slightest infection would be disastrous. We just can't allow anyone under ten years old into the ICU. No exceptions."

"How long?" I wrote quickly.

"A while. Two, or maybe three, months."

Some professional women see work and family as separate. I never have. My life is my family and always has been. I grew up in Cooper City, a suburb of Fort Lauderdale. In my teens, I knew two things: I wanted to be a marine biologist (my dad, a highway patrolman, and I got our scuba certifications together the summer I was fourteen); and I wanted to be a mother.

One day Mom—an amateur photographer—sent some vacation shots of me to a local modeling agency. The agency asked me to come in. The same year I got my scuba certification, I came to New York to shoot my first cover, for *Seventeen* magazine.

More work followed. At seventeen I was *Vogue's* youngest cover girl ever. I still loved the ocean, but marine biology wasn't to be. Being a mom was. I married at eighteen. A year later I gave birth to Hunter and Jake. A lot of folks thought I was crazy to have kids during my most lucrative modeling years. Couldn't I wait?

No. From the start, modeling had been a family affair for me. Either Mom or Dad or both of them always came with me on shoots. If a cameraman needed a hand moving some cable or a stylist needed someone to run out for two dozen gerbera daisies, my parents were ready to pitch in. My sisters, Joelle and Krissy, came along too, whenever they could. Now I had my boys to add to the mix.

I felt very, very blessed and very grateful. But there were clouds on the horizon, times ahead when I would need my faith more than ever. In 1995 my little sister, Krissy, died suddenly of right ventricular dysplasia, a rare heart condition. She was only seventeen. It devastated my parents and left a huge hole in our lives. In 1996 I went through a painful divorce. I'd always felt that everything in life happens for a reason, a reason that sometimes only God understands. Holding on to that belief became harder than I'd ever dreamed it could be.

And now here I was, flat on my back because of multiple surgeries, completely immobile, staring at the blank ceiling. Not see my kids for months? Hunter and Jake needed their mom. And I needed them. I needed all our little daily rituals: putting them into their PJs, picking up their toys, smelling their hair after a bath. At age six, life moves at a hundred miles an hour. They were making new discoveries, growing in new ways every day. How much of their lives had I missed already, just in the last month?

I got angry at the only one I knew could hear me. Staring up at that empty ceiling, I thought, *God, I know how fortunate I've been in my life, but I've had my heartbreaks too and I don't want anymore. All I want is to see my kids!*

Suddenly my mind flashed back to the accident. *I need to be okay for my kids.* That was it. That was the point. I would do whatever it took to get better, to survive this.

The next morning Mom walked in with a bunch of new photos of Hunter and Jake and thumb-tacked the pictures to the ceiling. My heart swelled with an aching joy. *Yes, Lord, I need to be okay for my kids. Thank You for the reminder.*

After a little more than a month, I was well enough to sit up. My world grew to include not just the ceiling plastered with pictures of Hunter and Jake, but the walls of my room. I could look straight at the doctors and my family, even if I still couldn't talk. And, for the first time, I could see the TV that hung over my bed.

Mom took advantage of that. She brought in a package. There was a video in it. She popped it in and suddenly my boys were there in front of me, moving and talking, horsing around for the camera, showing off their new toys. Telling me how much they missed me. How much they loved me.

It was the middle of July —two and a half months since the crash—when I finally got the word I'd been waiting for. "The risk of infection is down enough for us to move you across the street to the rehab hospital," one of my doctors said to me. "Better yet, your boys can see you."

I made the trip over later that day. First thing the next morning, the door opened and Hunter and Jake ran in. They were dressed in mini surgical scrubs. Each one even had a little stethoscope. They hopped up onto the bed and put their arms around me. I had a tube in my trachea, so I still couldn't talk—could barely move, in fact. For the rest of the day, they hung out with me in the bed and we watched TV together, just like we would have on a normal, lazy Saturday at home. I had my boys back at last. And I knew, somewhere inside, that things were going to be okay.

The road back was long and tough and painful. After dozens of operations to repair the damage of the accident, I had too many scars to be a full-body model anymore. But my face hadn't been touched. I would still be able to earn a good living in that profession, if I wanted to. But did I? So far I'd managed to navigate both the triumphs and the tragedies that came along because of the anchor provided by my family and my faith. If things really did happen for a reason, it was up to me to find the reason for my accident—to discover how I could turn what had happened to me into something genuinely positive.

I left the modeling world and started a brand-new chapter of my life in a brand-new place. I picked Nashville. I had fallen in love with it on a visit. I figured it was the perfect environment for my boys to grow up in. Underneath it all I'm still a tomboy. Here I have plenty of opportunity to let that out. I have a motorcycle, the boys have dirt bikes, and on any weekend you're likely to find us on them. And, of course, there's our church, Calvary Chapel Brentwood, where we feel at home every Sunday, a place where we can center our lives.

My manager, Lou Taylor, and I opened a clothing store in Nashville called Abbie & Jesse's (Abbie is Lou's dog and Jesse is mine), and I founded an organization that gives women with exciting business ideas but limited resources a chance to develop them. I called it the begin Foundation. (That's right, with a small "b" because the best things start out small.) Hunter and Jake are growing like crazy and I'm loving every minute of it. All I ever wanted was to see them again, to never miss another Mother's Day. This year, like every year since I left the hospital, it will be the happiest day of my life.

The Best Job

I'd rather be a mother than anyone on earth
Bringing up a child or two of unpretentious birth....
I'd rather wash a smudgy face with round, bright baby eyes—
Than paint the pageantry of fame, or walk among the wise.

MEREDITH GRAY

The Day Norman Rockwell Painted Mother

BY VIRGINIA MORTON

When I was ten years old Norman Rockwell lived in the town of my childhood, New Rochelle, New York. It was exciting, having a famous artist among us, and we children were intrigued by him. Knowing that Rockwell often used his neighbors as models for his paintings, we children speculated on the happy possibility that someone we knew might be chosen, at any moment, for fame and glory via the cover illustration of a national magazine.

Sometimes, after school, a group of us would take the longer road home, past Rockwell's house, deliberately dawdling and striking statuesque poses in the vain hope that the artist might look out his studio window and "discover" one of us.

One evening at dinner my mother calmly announced, as she served the peas, that she had received a telephone call from Norman Rockwell asking her to pose for him. I was stunned.

My mother! The very same mother I had been seeing every day of my life!

Until that moment I had never thought of Mother as anything but...Mother. Of course I loved her, and needed her, but mostly I regarded her as the ever-present, efficient supervisor of our household, who insisted that my clothes be hung up properly, my bed made smoothly, and my homework finished on time. She was a reliable housekeeper and cook, and a handy baker of cookies for Girl Scout gatherings—but, an artist's model? Never, in my wildest imaginings!

I began to look at this mother of mine more closely.

Mother was slim, I noted with some surprise, not quite so filled-out in the places where many mothers of the day were padded. Could it be that Mr. Rockwell admired her figure?

She had green eyes, which I knew, from bitter experience, could "see through" my childish evasions with alarming ease. Were they beautiful eyes? Mr. Rockwell might think so. I decided then and there that they must be beautiful.

Mother's hands were certainly familiar to me. They could soothe a flushed brow or paddle a youthful posterior with equal efficiency. Did Mr. Rockwell consider her hands noteworthy? I stared at the long, slim fingers, admired their grace; I hid my own grubby hands beneath my dinner napkin.

I studied Mother that evening as she continued to preside over the dinner table with her usual calm efficiency, apparently unaware of my close scrutiny. That evening I learned that my mother moved with grace, that she wore her clothes with a definite flair for style, that she had a delightful sense of humor, and laughed with an infectious gaiety all her own. Oh but it was exciting to find, so unexpectedly, a brand-new beautiful and charming mother in place of the one I had always taken so much for granted!

Mother was proud that she had been a registered nurse before she was married, and so was doubly pleased that she had been asked to pose as a nurse for Rockwell's painting.

When she returned from her first sitting, I threw myself into her arms and let fly a dozen questions at once. Mother laughed and hugged me. "It was great fun meeting Norman Rockwell," she said. "Why, he's so clever, he can paint, carry on a lively conversation, and keep up with the World Series on the radio, all at the same time!"

"Tell me about your picture," I begged. "Who are you supposed to be? What are you doing...?"

"We had lunch together," Mother said. "Tuna sandwiches and..."

"Oh Mother!" I protested. "It's the painting I want to hear about, not what you had for lunch! Will you be...beautiful?"

Mother smiled a rather strange and wistful smile. "The painting is to be a surprise, honey. You will see it for yourself when it comes out as a magazine cover in two months."

When you are only ten, two months can seem as long as a lifetime. The suspense was awful.

When the publishing date finally arrived, I hurried home from school to share Mother's moment of glory. I burst through the front door of our house and landed in the midst of a wild scene of hilarity.

There stood Mother, surrounded by friends and relatives, all shrieking with laughter over the magazine she held. Bewildered, I squeezed through for a closer look.

There was My Mother, for all the world to see, in full color, on the cover of one of America's most popular magazines. However, to my utter dismay she was not pictured as an ideal nurse, but as a caricature!

The illustration was of a nurse maid, sitting in a position of abject despair beside a howling baby. With cap askew, feet encased in ugly high-button shoes, scrawny elbows on knees and chin in hand, she rolled her eyes pleadingly heavenward in a scene of nightmare disorder.

I looked at the picture in horror. This wasn't my Mother the artist had painted! My Mother was beautiful, graceful, competent. This illustration was a mockery. I grabbed the magazine and before anyone could stop me, I tore up that cover.

It was some time before I could forgive Mr. Rockwell. But the passing years have softened that once-painful memory and eventually my hurt was replaced with an exciting discovery. My mother had become, through my imagining, all that I could ever hope her to be! I found that if I looked to her for understanding, sympathy, wisdom, humor...it was all there, ready to envelop me, guide me, and enrich my life. In trying to visualize her through an artist's eyes, seeking only beauty and perfection, I had stumbled upon a valuable truth: the eyes of love are creative, calling forth the best in the beloved, and seeing virtues that normal vision could never perceive.

Over the years I have felt a growing sense of gratitude to Norman Rockwell, for through him I came to see, really see, my mother.

Lingering Picture

Perchance the years have changed her.
Yet alone this picture lingers: still she seems
to me the fair, young angel of my infancy.

EDMUND CLARENCE STEDMAN

Little Smidgeons

BY PAULINE JENSEN

Whenever Tom, my brother, and I approached our home after school and sniffed the fragrance of fresh bread or of jellies in the making, Tom would wrinkle his nose. "Now, which one of us has to deliver a smidgeon?" he'd ask.

Sure enough, as soon as we entered the house Mother would look up. "I've a smidgeon of fresh rolls and blackberry jam that I want one of you to take to Emily Jones. Poor thing's been sick."

"You're not going to give the jam away?" Tom would protest. "You only made a little of it this year, with blackberries so scarce."

Mother would look at him long and hard. "It's only a smidgeon," she'd say, "and I'm sure the rest will taste better, knowing that Emily Jones is enjoying this jar."

We learned early in life to accept Mother's attitude on giving.

One Christmas morning Mother learned that the Barkley family had received nothing for Christmas. Mr. Barkley had left the family and Mrs. Barkley had no money.

"Now, let's see," Mother said, casting an appraising look over our Christmas haul, "there ought to be something those children could use."

In the end Tom and I gave up a portion of our gifts.

"You can't use two baseballs," Mother said to Tom. "And it wouldn't look right giving an old one for Christmas." With resignation. Tom laid the new baseball in the basket Mother was filling. "And that hair ribbon," Mother addressed me, "would look very pretty on the littlest Barkley girl."

However, Mother didn't ask us to sacrifice alone. "I'll just send this mince pie along," she said.

"That only leaves one pie and with four Campbells coming we'll be seven," Tom complained.

"I don't want any," Mother's voice was brusque. "I don't have an appetite for mince pie right now."

Tom and I looked at one another, remembering that just a week ago Mother had said, "I never seem to get enough mince pie."

When the Depression came, Tom and I were both married and Mother lived alone. When the firm in which she had her life's savings fell, she was left with barely enough to get by on. Tom and I supplemented that with what we could spare.

"I like to think of her being able to buy ice cream and an occasional magazine," Tom said.

One afternoon when I dropped in on her unexpectedly, I saw her talking to a stranger, a door-to-door salesman. She had not seen me, so I stepped back beside the house.

"I don't need a thing," Mother said, "but here's a smidgeon of cash. Fifty cents will buy your family two dozen eggs and some bacon."

When I told Tom about it later, he asked, "Did you say anything to her?"

I shook my head. "What good would it do?"

Mother's smidgeons didn't always consist of food or money. When the Hartfords lost their little girl, Mother was the first to go to them.

After her heart attack, we tried to keep a watchful eye upon her, but it proved difficult. Tom dropped in one morning to find her hanging out a washing—not her own.

He confronted her sternly.

"Now, what's your excuse?"

"Well, Lily Andrews has the flu and with all those small children, she needed a few things washed."

"But you're not supposed to do washing," Tom stormed.

Mother looked up at him, quietly.

"Tom, there's only two things I've asked of the Lord: to serve Him daily and, when my time comes, to go without any fuss, right in my own bed. I've a feeling He's going to allow me both those things."

In her brief illness, before she did go "without any fuss," she fretted about the medical bills.

"I wanted to leave you a smidgeon of cash," she once told us.

We tried to make her understand that it didn't matter. Gently Tom took her hand. "You're leaving us far more than any cash. We had to grow up and become parents before we learned that you didn't give things—you shared them! Anyone can give if he has the means, but few people ever learn to share."

I patted her thin cheeks. "You see, Mother, all those smidgeons left an indelible mark upon us."

She leaned back against the pillows, a smile hovering around the corners of her mouth...a little smidgeon of a smile.

Mother's Math

A mother is a person who seeing there are only four pieces of pie for five people, promptly announces she never did care for pie.

TENNEVA JORDAN

Mother's Strength

BY MARIA MASSEI-ROSATO

The night before Mother's Day last year, a night warmed by the first breath of summer, I gave my four-month-old son his usual bedtime bath. As I drew the soapy washcloth down his back, starting from the tender spot at the nape of his neck, Anthony let out a sigh as if that were the moment he'd been waiting for all day. Then he gazed up at me, curiosity and trust in his big blue eyes.

I couldn't help but think of the different look I'd gotten from the other person I had bathed that night, just an hour earlier—his grandma, my seventy-five-year-old mother, Josephine. When I'd touched the washcloth to her skin, her expression had clouded with fear, suspicion, and anger. No relaxing ritual, that bath had been more of a battle. In the five years since her diagnosis, Alzheimer's had changed my mom into a frail, childlike woman who needed constant supervision. Still, bathtime often sparked her old independence. "Get away from me," she'd snapped when I leaned over the tub in the house where I grew up. "I'll do it."

I'll do it. How many times had I heard her say that over the years? "Don't worry, I'll do it. I'll take care of it," Mom would tell me, her voice as strong and sure as she herself seemed, down to her very core. Though motherhood came to my mom late in life—my parents adopted my brother and me when she was close to forty—it was like second nature to her. She was blessed with enough maternal instincts to take care of a whole bunch of kids, and that's exactly what she did after my father died when I was ten. Mom took up work as a baby-sitter and later as a seamstress in our Brooklyn neighborhood to support us. She went on raising us as if she hadn't had a question in her mind as to whether she could do it on her own. Even after we lost my brother to drugs, I felt as though nothing could ever really break my mother's spirit and defeat her.

I could use some of that strength, I thought, resting my elbows on the edge of the tub while Anthony splashed. Mom's and my roles were reversing and it was my turn to look after her, to give back a little of what she gave me, but my mind was flooded with questions and doubts. *God, my baby needs me. So does my mom—more than ever. How will I take good care of both of them at the same time? I'm not sure I can do all this.*

And the next day was Mother's Day. "We have to do something special," my husband Tony had insisted. "This is your first one." But it felt strange, almost wrong, to celebrate when my own mother was drifting away, becoming someone I didn't know.

Mom used to make me beautiful outfits to wear to church on Easter, dresses with satin sashes and matching bonnets, every stitch sewn by hand. Now she couldn't even button her grandson's sweater or tie his shoes. She used to want to handle everything herself. When we had company for dinner, she'd clean until the house was spotless. She'd see to every detail of the meal down to the grated Locatelli cheese in her famous meatballs, and make sure her guests didn't want for anything. Now she was oddly docile, content for the most part to let other people do the cooking and cleaning and look after her. Except for those flashes of anger and mistrust that so upset me, like during her bath.

For months, she had hid the ominous signs. She'd joke with her next-door neighbor Diana about getting to a certain age and having too many memories to keep track of. She'd walk in and out of the kitchen countless times, forgetting what she was looking for. I finally convinced her to see a doctor. By that point, though, I don't think Mom was able to understand the profound implications of her diagnosis.

But somewhere deep in that core of strength she'd always had, she sensed something was wrong, and she tried to hold off the encroaching mental fog with every ounce of dignity she had. I tried too, for as long as I could, to minimize the inroads Alzheimer's made on our lives. But I didn't think I was as strong as she was.

To some degree, I should have known what to expect. For two years, I'd volunteered in a day-care program for people with Alzheimer's that provided a respite for their primary caregivers.

I had signed up after Mom's diagnosis, thinking the work was a way to prepare for my eventual role. It had been hard to see those people failing, their minds taken over by that fog that rolled in and never went away. Still, their needs had seemed simple enough to fulfill. One man just wanted me to help him with his jigsaw puzzle; one of the women liked to sing the same song time after time.

It was only when my mother's Alzheimer's began to take over her personality that I realized nothing about the disease was simple at all. The more lost Mom became, the more I found myself turning to prayer, although I struggled for words so often I worried that God wouldn't understand my awkward requests.

I talked to Mom every day, and fortunately my company allowed me to scale back to a part-time work schedule, so I could be with her more. We didn't do anything extraordinary—played rummy, went shopping, grabbed a couple of slices at her favorite pizza place down the block—but those days together were special just the same. *God, this time while Mom still knows what's going on... still knows me*, I prayed, *help me make the most of it.*

Gradually I took over doing things Mom used to do for herself. First, paying her bills, then scheduling her doctor's appointments and taking her to them, doing her grocery shopping and taking her to the hairdresser. Our friend and neighbor Diana was wonderful with her. She checked in on my mother regularly and treated her as lovingly as if she were her own.

Mom fought to hold onto her independence for all she was worth, and sometimes that meant fighting me. "Why are you doing this to me?" she'd screamed one afternoon when I asked her to wait while I bought a book on the way back from her doctor's appointment. "You only care about yourself!" Trying to ignore the stares from the other customers, I paid for my book and hurried Mom back to the house.

That night I called my friend Yvonne, the volunteer who'd shown me the ropes at the respite program. She was a reluctant expert, having lost her mother to Alzheimer's. "You can't take it personally," Yvonne told me. "Your mom's not really mad at you. She's frustrated that she can't do what she used to. And she's frightened. Just give her some space."

As my mother deteriorated, I kept asking Yvonne for advice. She warned me that even everyday things would take a lot more preparation, that I would have to think through every step and figure out how to get Mom to do what she needed to do.

The low-key Mother's Day celebration my husband had urged, for example, I'd planned several weeks ahead. Tony and I thought we would pick up Mom, go to church, then have a barbecue in our backyard. We invited Diana, but she was going on vacation and couldn't make it. "Your mom's going to need a bath by then, and you know how she kicks and screams. I feel bad I won't be around to help," Diana said.

The closer we got to Mother's Day weekend, the more tense I grew about bathing Mom. That Friday, Hazel, a volunteer in a program sponsored by my mother's health insurance company, made her weekly visit, and seeing Mom's face light up when her friend walked in, I remembered the first time Hazel had come by two years earlier. People with Alzheimer's don't deal with change well, and I'd worried about how Mom would react to a stranger in her house. But Mom took to Hazel right away. She actually played the hostess, poured tea, and brought out canned peaches, her favorite, for her guest. "Hot tea and sliced peaches, not a great combination," I'd remarked to Hazel later. "That's okay," she replied. "It makes your mom feel good to do this for me." Even though Hazel had to help feed Mom the peaches now, her visits always put Mom in a good mood.

Saturday evening I headed over to give Mom the dreaded bath, wishing I had more of Hazel's understanding, Diana's resilience, and Yvonne's compassion. *Please, God, help me*, I prayed. *I don't think I can do this.*

I parked out front and sat in my car for a moment, looking at the house where my mother had raised me. The brown shingles and the front porch with its painted columns were so familiar to me. So too was the light glowing in the living room window.

I remembered how Mom always used to leave the light on so I could get home safe and sound, and I felt comforted, as if God had given me a sign. *"Don't worry,"* I sensed Him telling me, *"I will guide your way and help you care for your mother. I'll be with both of you."*

Warmed by more than the whisper of summer in the air, I went inside and got Mom ready for her bath. "You want to look your best for Mother's Day, don't you?" I asked. With less protest than I'd expected, she stepped into the tub. I brought two washcloths, so we could share the job. Mom would have none of it. "Go away," she cried, swatting at my hands. "I'll do it."

"Wait till you see Anthony. He's getting so big," I said, distracting her. But washing her hair was more than she could take. When the water dripped down her face, she put her hands to her ears and opened her mouth. The scream that emerged seemed to come from the depths of her soul and reach the depths of mine. "I've done everything for you, and this is how you treat me? You don't know how much I love you!" she wailed.

Oh, Mom, I wish you could understand how much I love you, I thought as my mother looked heavenward and cried, "God, help me!"

"He is," I tried to tell her, but nothing I said could soothe her.

After Mom got in bed, I stayed with her until she drifted off. Watching the calm of sleep settle over her, I wondered, *Does she still know to turn to God?* Then I recalled a time she'd gone for a walk not long ago in our church garden and had dropped to her knees. No one could make out the words she'd murmured, but it had been clear to me that she was praying to God.

Prayer isn't about words, I realized. It's about trust—trust that God understands what we need and how we feel. Gratitude swept over me. Despite the ravages of Alzheimer's, the memories that had faded, my mother's faith remained, her core of strength now as always. "Good night, Ma," I whispered, kissing her on the forehead. "I'll see you tomorrow." I went home to bathe another person I love beyond description, my son.

As I squeezed the washcloth and let the water trickle down my baby's skin, he giggled just like he did whenever his grandma kissed his cheek, and at last I saw how I could look after both of them. At last I understood that God constantly works—with us and through us—to give us the compassion and strength we need to take care of one another. Mom and I would continue to face Alzheimer's together, guided and sustained by a faith anchored in prayer, a faith that I hoped to pass on to my son. I looked forward to celebrating that on my first Mother's Day.

Let God Take It

*Because God is responsible for our welfare,
we are told to cast all our care upon Him, for He
cares for us (1 Peter 5:7). God says, "I'll take the
burden—don't give it a thought—leave it to Me."
God is keenly aware that we are dependent
upon Him for life's necessities.*

BILLY GRAHAM

Lauren's Dream

BY LAURA WRAY

The school bus pulled up on our block and Lauren skipped to the front door, her wheat-colored curls bouncing. "Look, Mom!" she shouted, waving a sheet of paper at me. CHEERLEADER TRYOUTS! read the heading. "I'm going to be a cheerleader!" she yelled. But my eighteen-year-old daughter wasn't like the other girls who waved pompoms at Verden High School basketball games. Lauren has Down syndrome.

My stomach was in knots, just like when she'd signed up for the girls' softball team or to sing in the youth choir at our small-town church. But this was worse. Cheerleaders commanded individual attention. Lauren couldn't blend into the back row. What if the other girls on the squad didn't accept her? What if people made fun of her? What if she got hurt? I put my hand on her shoulder and we walked to the kitchen for a snack. "Lauren," I said calmly, "you're involved in so much already with church, school, and sports. Don't you think that's enough?"

She crossed her arms and frowned. "Mom, I want to be a cheerleader."

"I know, sweetie, but..." my voice trailed off. "Let's pass on cheerleading." I searched her face to make sure she understood.

Lauren finished her apple slices and milk, then raced out of the kitchen to watch TV. I was relieved that my decision didn't seem to devastate her. That night, I told my husband, Johnny, about this latest challenge. Our prayer since Lauren's birth had been that she'd reach her full potential, be as independent as possible and lead a happy life. She was doing great. Still, I felt extremely protective.

The next day Lauren handed me a note about cheerleading uniforms. "I thought we decided that you didn't have time for cheerleading," I said.

"I'm already a cheerleader!" she said, grinning. "Mrs. Pettit said I could." When Lauren set her mind to do something, she didn't give up easily. Still, I couldn't imagine Lauren out there on the court. So public. So vulnerable. I knew what was best for her, and this definitely wasn't it. "With your other activities, you can't handle this," I said firmly.

Lauren's expression shifted. Her mouth turned downward and her bottom lip stuck out. We stood there, silent. Slowly, she lifted her gaze. "I can handle it," she whispered, her eyes fixed on mine.

Lauren was more determined than I'd thought. I shouldn't have been surprised. We'd mainstreamed her since kindergarten so she wouldn't feel different. If Lauren really wanted to be a cheerleader, could I stand in her way? Wouldn't it be hypocritical?

I thought back to when the test confirmed that Lauren had Down syndrome. Anguish surged through me when I considered all that Lauren would never experience—college, marriage, children. I'd felt so helpless. I had to put my trust in God. Now, in so many ways, she was living the life I'd dreamed she'd live: playing sports, hanging out with friends, feeling proud and independent. Why wasn't I happy for her?

I barely got an hour's worth of sleep that night. Images haunted me: pompoms swishing beside pleated crimson skirts. Strangers laughing. Lauren looking sad, wishing she'd never become a cheerleader....

The next afternoon, I parked in front of the school gym and went in to watch practice. Girls in T-shirts and shorts turned cartwheels across the hardwood floor, ponytails flying. They were rehearsing a complicated dance routine. As I settled into the bleachers, I spotted Lauren standing alone on the sidelines. Her short legs and stout torso hampered her running and jumping ability. Yet after each of the other girls' leaps, Lauren hollered, "Woo hoo!"

Afterward, I told Johnny how Lauren cheered for the other cheerleaders instead of practicing the routine. "I don't think Lauren understood," I said.

"We've always prayed that Lauren would lead as normal a life as possible," he reminded me. "This is important to her. We have to trust God that it will work out." Johnny was right. Lauren was growing up. Next year, she'd graduate. I'd need to trust God more than ever. But that's the hardest thing of all—to trust your children to God, especially a child like Lauren.

The day of the first basketball game arrived. I couldn't concentrate at all. I paced back and forth in the kitchen. "Nervous?" I asked, as we drove to the gym.

"Nope," replied Lauren. "It'll be a blast!"

I had enough anxiety for us both. I wasn't sure if Lauren could handle being in front of a big crowd. Sometimes she did unexpected things, like when she walked out of church, distracted, in the middle of a choir performance. What if something like that happened today? There was a major dance routine at the half. Every eye in the gym would be on her.

The buzzer squawked. Halftime. The basketball team dashed toward the locker room as the cheerleaders sprinted onto center court. Their excitement shook the stands. Lauren smiled as she thrust her pompoms to her hips, waiting for the CD to begin. I bit my bottom lip. I watched her begin to move to the loud, driving music.

Lauren's timing was off. Her jumps weren't as high as the other girls'. Yes, people were staring. But not because she was awkward. Her big brown eyes sparkled, as though illuminated from within. She wasn't keeping up, but the smile on her face told me—and everyone—she was having the time of her life. Somehow, with all my worry, I'd failed to notice that glow, her sheer exuberance. Lauren was a cheerleader. Why hadn't I been cheering for her? If I trusted God, then I needed to trust Him with everything, especially Lauren. Not just in cheerleading, but in life.

Okay, Lord, I'm letting go and letting you take care of Lauren—right now, I prayed.

The routine ended and the crowd erupted in applause. Neighbors who'd watched Lauren grow up dabbed their eyes. Classmates she'd known since kindergarten looked so proud. I watched my daughter take a jubilant bow. Moments later, she bounded into the bleachers. "Hi, Mom!" she said, wiping sweat from her face. "Did you see me? It was fun!"

"Yes, Honey," I replied and hugged her tight. "Way to go, Lauren!" the people sitting behind us called out to her. I loosened my grip, and Lauren started down the steps, while other fans shouted words of encouragement. "You go, girl!" "Great job!" A few students sitting in the aisle raised up their hands for high fives as Lauren made her way back down to the court. She was ready to cheer some more. So was I.

Biggest Cheerleader

*Encouragement is awesome. It has the
capacity to...spark the flicker of a smile on the
face of a discouraged child. To breathe fresh fire
into the fading embers of a smoldering dream.
To actually change the course of another
human being's day, week, or life.*

CHARLES R. SWINDOLL

My Mom's Best Recipes

BY ANDRA OLENIK

When I left San Diego to go to college in New York City, it never occurred to me how far away I'd truly be. But Mom knew. She also knew I'd get hungry for home cooking. So, along with the extra-long sheets for my dorm bed and warm clothes for northeast winters, she tucked into my suitcase a one-of-a-kind cookbook—a journal in which she'd handwritten the recipes for my favorite dishes, at least the ones that were easy enough for a beginner and could be made in an ill-equipped starter kitchen. Mom even illustrated the recipes: a smiling Humpty Dumpty for Gratin of Eggs, a plump little fruit for Glazed Apples, a tasty bird on a platter for her Sunday Roast Chicken.

Though college was a time of growing up, these recipes brought me back to my childhood, and to Mom. Recipes like Tommy Brock's Wheat Germ Muffins—my fiancé Jon's favorite—from *Peter Rabbit's Natural Foods Cookbook*. Mom and I first cooked together from that book, making Samuel Whiskers's Roly-Poly Pancakes on weekend mornings. "Crack the eggs in there," she'd say, pointing to an orange bowl. She'd let me measure the dry ingredients, using a knife to level off the flour. I'd stand at her side, my nose barely clearing the counter, while Mom mixed it then poured the batter into shapes. "Do you want Mickey Mouse or a flower?" My brother usually wanted a train or a truck. Mom always rose to the challenge.

It wasn't until after college that I discovered something amazing about Mom: she didn't always know how to cook. What?! The mother I knew made elaborate meals for every occasion! On weekends we had friends over for barbecue—chicken, legs of lamb, whole turkeys. Then there was the lobster bake, when the live crustaceans escaped their bag in the fridge so that when we opened the door they fell onto the floor and started crawling. We kids ran away squealing. Mom made poached salmon for Easter, an Indian curry feast for her book club, and every year dozens of guests devoured her Oysters Rockefeller at our Christmas party. And this woman wasn't born cooking? I couldn't believe it. "Is it true you couldn't cook?" I asked Mom.

"When I was first married, I had no idea," she said, "but I watched Julia Child on TV and worked my way through her book *The Art of French Cooking*." Mom learned techniques she could apply to anything. She still proudly brandishes the well-loved cookie sheet Julia herself—a guest teacher at a cooking class Mom took—used to bake palmiers. "Everything I bake on this turns out perfect," Mom says. (It does!)

The pages of the recipe book Mom made me are stained now, the illustrations smudged, her beautiful handwriting offset by my own less elegant scrawl, where I've added new recipes. Messiest of all is the recipe for her Sunday Roast Chicken, which I make when a friend comes over for a girl's night. We chat about our lives, our loves, our families—and our moms. We grab each end of the wishbone—something Mom used to save for my brother and me—and make a wish. When I was little I'd wish for a Barbie Dream House. Later on, I'd wish for a man who'd love me forever. I finally found him, and the first time I invited Jon over for dinner, I fixed—of course—Sunday Roast Chicken.

I cook for friends, for family, for Jon, but I'll always think of myself as Mom's sous chef. She still teaches me techniques, and every now and then I teach her something too. But the biggest thing I've learned is that cooking is how we take care of the people we love. It's how Mom always took care of me, even thousands of miles from home.

Mom's Kitchen

*Every family has those recipes that are
associated with home. Those dishes that
your mom prepared that everyone loves, those
are your comfort foods. Those are the recipes that
are taken to potlucks, passed around and handed
down to the next generation. When you smell
them cooking it takes you back to Mom's
kitchen. No one can cook like Mom!*

DIANNE LOOMOS

Come Live with Us

BY DOROTHY DEBOLT

We were playing in the back yard, and I said to my adopted son, "Marty, will you please go get the newspaper on the front lawn?" He turned and took a few steps. Then he froze. Suddenly he was in my arms, sobbing.

I knew that Marty was a frightened little boy, but I hadn't known that he had developed such a dependence on me. He was an American-Korean orphan and had been found in a gutter in Seoul at the age of six months. He had been raised in an orphanage where there was not enough staff with enough time to give him enough love. He came to us when he was almost three, tiny and terrified.

My family had enough love for Marty to overcome his fears. But, even at three, Marty sensed that there was no permanence in his life, and he felt secure in our love only when we were within touch. I knew he had to overcome this so that he could have a normal life.

So I made a game out of it. Each day I asked Marty to go and get the paper. Each day he was able to go a few steps farther. Finally, after months, he made it. As he came running back to me with the paper, I saw his tears, but he was also grinning. And when he threw himself into my arms, I felt his tremors of joy and triumph.

I could share this joy with Marty because I had experienced it myself, although in a different way. It was morning, I remember, just after breakfast, and I was in the kitchen, ready to do the dishes. My husband passed through the room on his way to the car. He stopped and kissed me, winked and grinned and said, "Hold the fort." Then he left.

Our first child was crawling on the kitchen floor; our second child was in her crib; our third child was alive within me, kicking occasionally to affirm her presence. I glanced out the window. The cherry trees were in blossom. The lemon trees were full of promise.

Suddenly a jolt of happiness shot through me. For the first time in my life I was aware of the presence of God, right there in the kitchen with me. I felt fulfilled, completed, joyful. My eyes filled. I whispered, "Thank You, God. Thank You for all of this. Thank You for so much love." I don't know how long I stood there, enraptured.

Later, when I tried to convey the experience to my father, all I could say was, "It was like being on some artificial high, Dad, but I know it was of God."

Dad nodded. "I'm sure it was," he said. "And you did the right thing in acknowledging it and thanking Him. But we must remember, Dorothy, that God is also with us at times of sorrow.

God allows us to learn from sorrow. People forget that. When sorrow strikes, they think God has abandoned them and they challenge Him."

I wasn't sure what he meant. I asked, "Dad, does God test us?"

"No," he said. "Life does. But God is always there."

I learned the truth in that. The joy I had felt that morning sustained me through the sorrow when, a year later, I stood by helplessly while my father died, slowly and painfully, from cancer. I waited for the familiar surge of resentment, the *Why my father, Lord? Why me?* Instead, what passed through my mind was, *I thank You for this experience, Lord. Show me what You want me to learn from it.*

The joy sustained me again when, after another year and during my fifth pregnancy, I suffered a miscarriage and the doctors advised me against having any more children for a while. Disappointed, I could only pray, *Lord, if You have a plan for me, if there is anything I am to learn from this, please show me.*

It was out of our prayers that, almost simultaneously, the thought struck Ted and me that we should adopt some children, and we particularly wanted Korean orphans. For us the decision was a way of expressing our gratitude to God for His many blessings. We got in touch with the appropriate agencies and began the ordeal of waiting.

Ted and I and our four children were at the San Francisco airport getting our first look at Marty as he came off the plane.

That great joy of God's presence filled me as I kissed Marty for the first time, and Ted said softly, "I wish he were twins. Let's get some more."

Two years later we did—Kim, who was then six years old. Soon his laughter was everywhere in our house.

Just six short years later life tested me again. Ted, under fifty, developed a brain tumor and died. Perhaps if I had not known God's presence in joys, He might not have been enough for me in this great sorrow, and it was knowing this that kept me going.

I had taught music, so I went back to that, and my earnings, in addition to what Ted had left me, enabled me to keep my family together. To keep busy, we formed a singing group and sang at churches and on television. I knew I wasn't the only young widow with children; I felt I could learn something from friendships with other such women, and so I became active in Parents Without Partners. In time, I realized, I might marry again. However, with seven children in the house, I did not expect any rush of suitors.

I received a call from the Committee of Responsibility, a group of doctors, clergymen, and laymen organized to bring badly injured South Vietnamese children to this country for medical treatment. I learned about two boys, both fourteen, who needed a home until they could be returned to Vietnam. They were both paraplegic. I said I would have to talk to my children.

I did, and Marty asked, "What's a paraplegic?"

"Someone paralyzed from the waist down," I answered.

"Then they'll need a lot of people to take care of them. Let them live with us, Mom," Marty replied.

Thus Tich and Anh moved in. When we learned that their families had died in the war, I adopted them. They got a lot of care, mostly from the children. Soon they were able to get about in wheelchairs. Later they were able to go to school; finally they were able to walk on crutches.

That same year I met Bob DeBolt, a San Francisco engineer, who was divorced and raising a daughter. After a friendship of several months Bob asked me to marry him. I said, "Bob, you must be crazy. I've got nine kids from all over the world, two of them handicapped, and one more is on the way from Biafra."

"That doesn't bother me," Bob said easily. "What bothers me is, what have you got against Mexican Americans and Native Americans?"

We were married in June a year later, and our wedding vows included a special promise that we would always welcome into our hearts and home anybody who wished to enter. We have kept that vow.

Looking back, we all got along with blessed ease. Each child had chores that kept the house in order. My big job was the cooking. One summer most of our vegetables came from the garden Tich and Anh cultivated in the back yard. By the age of sixteen, each child was expected to find a part-time job to cover his personal expenses, allowing Bob and me to use our incomes to support the younger children. Upon graduation from high school, each child was expected to make his own way through college, if that's what he wanted, or his own place in the business world, moving out of the house to make room for new children.

At dinner, the only meal we all had together, we began with a thanksgiving to God for all He had given us, the children taking turns at the prayer. After dinner some of us read, some played games, most of us had a sing-along. Some nights I worked on my book encouraging adoption; Bob spent many evenings keeping all the immigration forms up to date. From time to time, a child from another land told us about the customs of his country and his religion, which taught the children that they are brothers and sisters not only through adoption but also through natural love in the family of man.

One October Bob and I welcomed into our home our fifteenth child, Karen, just six, an African-American girl from New York, who was a congenital amputee with only partial arms and no legs, a child who had lived unwanted in a hospital since birth.

When Bob and I first heard of Karen, we both sensed that God wanted her to join our family, but we let the children decide. They put together a book of pictures of all of us and a letter from each child telling Karen why they felt she would be happy with us.

The day Karen entered our home was, for me, like the day Marty arrived, a day brought vividly to life by the joyful presence of God, a loving presence that, I have learned, can also be with us during our sorrows, not only to soothe us but also to guide us.

The Miracle of Family

*We witness a miracle every
time a child enters into life.
But those who make their journey
home across time and miles,
growing within the hearts of those
who wait to love them,
are...placed among us by God's
very own hands.*

KRISTI LARSON

That's My Mom!

BY ARTHUR A. GUENTHER

How do I remember my mother, Minnie Guenther, the "ninety-pound weakling" who not only reared nine children of her own but who has cared for hundreds more since 1911 on the Fort Apache Indian Reservation in Arizona?

The story really begins over fifty years ago before I was born. Mother met my father, Edgar Guenther, at choir practice one night in 1907 when they lived in Milwaukee. He was in a Lutheran seminary. Mom was a secretary.

It took Dad four years to get around to a proposal, and it was an odd one at that. Mother was on her way out one day when he came dashing up to the house and blurted out, "I've just accepted a call as a missionary to the Apache Indians in Arizona. Will you go with me?"

They left for Arizona the day after they were married, carting all their worldly goods with them: a cookstove, some clothes, their Bible, a few other volumes, and a mail-order medical book.

Their first home consisted of two drab rooms of a four-room frame building on the east fork of the White River, the fledgling mission of the Wisconsin Lutheran Synod. Back in 1911 Arizona was not yet a state, only a territory. Mother went to work.

She learned to ride a horse so she could accompany her husband on his camp visits up and down the valleys and mountains of the 1,666,000-acre reservation. They both learned the Apache language and Mother taught herself to play the piano and a small portable organ for church services. In her tiny quarters she held Sunday school and Bible classes for more years than I can remember.

During the epidemic that took a terrible toll of life, especially among the children, she learned how to nurse. "It's remarkable," she says, "how much therapy there is in castor oil, epsom salts, skunk oil, axle grease, honey and water, flannel blankets, bed sheets torn into bandages, a pat on the head...and love."

My parents were horrified to discover that the Apaches considered it an evil omen when twins or a deformed child were born. The practice was to kill one of the twins and all the disfigured babies. Mother took many such children into her home. She just started an orphanage. The first child slept in an apple box in a corner of one of their two rooms. From this humble beginning an orphanage was established that became an institution caring for children from broken homes and poor families. In a span of twenty-five years 980 babies were provided for.

Six months after they arrived Father built some desks and benches; Mother typed copy after copy of "textbooks" for reading, writing, arithmetic, and religion; then she started a school in her house with sixteen children. She fed them a hot meal at noon and also taught the girls how to sew, bake bread, and raise vegetables.

This school became a big, beautiful building with 285 children and classes from kindergarten through high school.

Mother did all these things while she raised her own family. She had nine children, all born without benefit of doctor or hospital. When the first baby was arriving, Father reached for the home medical book and yelled, "Quick, Minnie. Read what I have to do." Mother couldn't find the place, so Father grabbed a passing cowboy, who officiated. After that Father was the midwife.

They also reared two Apache girls and a boy from early childhood. They were our sisters and brother, living with us, sharing our food and our faith. One of my Apache sisters later died. Mother raised her son. The Apaches grew to love Mother so much they called her "Shemah." It means "my mother."

When the World War I hysteria broke out against people with German names, the army arrested my father and put him in the Fort Apache guardhouse. Mother was left alone to give birth to her fourth child. Her faith never faltered.

How she ever managed to stretch my father's sixty dollars a month to feed and clothe us all still escapes me. But there was always enough food and we had a large garden. Even during the Depression, when people fled the dust bowls and passed through our town of Whiteriver, Arizona, on their way to California, Mother had food to share with them.

"We will just put another bean in the pot," she would say.

With Mother's help Father built four churches around Whiteriver. Once he was offered a language professorship at a college. He preferred to remain on the reservation, despite the hardships. I know that many times he would have despaired had it not been for the strength of my mother. The right word at the proper time. A smile. An admonition.

My parents did their work well. All my sisters became wives and mothers; one was a nurse; two were teachers. Of my brothers: Edgar was an army colonel in charge of training at Fort Sam Houston; Roland was a sales and service manager of International Harvester in South Dakota; Jonathan was an engineer in Tucson; and I was a pastor on the reservation, trying to follow in my father's way—and my mother's.

At seventy-seven Mother was still working. Every week she visited the hospital and daily held open house for a stream of Native Americans who looked to her to resolve all their heartaches: a quarreling couple; a drunken husband; a hungry family; a child who needed help to go to school. No one but me knew that out of her meager income she helped one girl become a nurse.

For her last birthday she wanted, of all things, a jungle gym. She put it in the playground across the street from my church.

At the last count, Mother had four great-grandchildren and twenty-two grandchildren. She and Father sent all their children to college. If asked how she managed her family, her answer is a message for today and for all time:

"Feed them, love them, give them a good Christian foundation, mix it all with discipline, and you can bet they'll build well on that."

A Mother's Strength

The very word "motherhood" has an emotional depth and significance few terms have. It bespeaks nourishment and safety and sheltering arms.

MARJORIE HOLMES

"Lord, Keep My Kids Safe"

BY MAE BERTHA CARTER

I woke up that September morning so filled with fear I could barely get out of bed. Matthew, my husband, was already up. He had fetched water from the pump, heated it up on the stove, and was filling the tub in the bedroom. Our five older children washed and got dressed while Matthew bathed our two youngest girls. I cooked breakfast. The kids were unusually quiet, no one talking excitedly about the first day of school. But then, school usually started for them in November, after most of the cotton had been picked.

Out of a wadded handkerchief I took seven quarters for lunch money and gave one to each of them—Deborah, Beverly, Pearl, Gloria, Stanley, Larry, and Ruth. Then we waited on the front porch for the school bus.

Normally they would have been out in the cotton fields working. We worked from "can to can't," sunrise to sunset. Other families stopped picking on Fridays at noon. Not us Carters. We worked right through the weekend until Saturday night: four bales a week. Even after school, if there was any cotton left, the children picked. But I had decided I didn't want them stuck in a sharecropper's life.

I finally spotted the school bus coming our way. Not a rusty old hand-me-down, but a brand-new yellow school bus. It stopped in front of our house. My kids were the first on. How would the other children react when they saw them there?

The fear came over me again. I watched the bus disappear down the road, then I went inside and lay across our bed. *Lord,* I prayed, *take care of my kids. Take care of my kids. Take care of my kids.* There have been times when I have felt God's covering, when I've sensed a protective peace all around. This time was not one of them. My children had gone off to school. The only black children to enter a white school in Drew, Mississippi.

In 1965 the local school board—under court order—instituted something called freedom of choice. That summer, when the cotton wasn't open yet, and the only work we had to do was tend our own vegetable garden, I was off visiting relatives in St. Louis the day the choice notices arrived at the farm. My girl Ruth opened the letter and made up her mind right away. She wanted to go to the white school. She talked to the other kids and one by one they came to the same decision. All Matthew and I could say was, "If you want to go, we want you to go."

Early on August 12, Matthew and I put on our best clothes, climbed into our pickup, and drove the nine miles into Drew. The town was quiet, but I felt as if everyone were peeking out of their windows at us. We stopped at the white high school, which was clean and freshly painted. It was the first time I had ever been inside. A secretary showed us into the principal's office. When we handed him the papers he got all red and flustered but didn't say anything. We had no idea we were the only black parents in the county who had chosen to desegregate a school.

Word got out. The next day the plantation overseer, Mr. Thornton, drove up. "It's starting," Matthew muttered as he headed outside. I overheard Mr. Thornton telling my husband our kids could get a better education at the black school, and the white kids wouldn't talk to them, and black folks wouldn't have anything to do with us either.

I got so riled up I went inside, picked up a portable record player, and a record my oldest son had given me of a President Kennedy speech about civil rights. I set the player on a chair near the door and turned the volume up so Mr. Thornton could hear Mr. Kennedy saying, "We are confronted primarily with a moral issue. It is as old as the Scriptures and is as clear as the American Constitution." We would not back down.

A few nights later Matthew was awakened at 3:00 a.m. by the sound of crunching gravel. He looked out the front window. "What on earth?" he muttered. The next thing I knew I was jolted out of bed by the *pop-pop-pop* of gunfire. *Lord, have mercy*. Bullets flew across the porch, shattering the windows. Bullets hit the wall above the bed where two of the kids were asleep. Scrambling through the house, Matthew and I brought all the kids to the back room. There we lay on the floor out of sight. The cars roared off, but we stayed put until dawn while Matthew sat by the front door, his shotgun in his lap.

I didn't know where to turn. I didn't feel I could trust any folk of authority in Drew. I had my husband drive me to Cleveland, the next town over, and I spoke to Mr. Moore, the head of the NAACP there. He notified the deputy sheriff of the county, and the FBI visited and took the bullets out of our walls as evidence. They promised there would be an investigation. But how would we sleep knowing someone wanted to do us harm?

The next night we returned to the back room, all of us huddled on the floor. I prayed and prayed for the Lord's covering. *Lord, keep my kids safe.* I also prayed, *Lord, help us eat.* That same day Matthew had gone to the country store, the only place we could buy on credit when we needed it. The manager took one look at my husband and said, "I'll give you until three o'clock to get your children out of the white school." When Matthew came home I dug out the forty dollars I had saved under our mattress, so he could shop at another store. How much longer could we survive?

For four nights we slept in the back room, me worrying myself sick. Then one evening I recalled something I once heard a preacher say: "Everybody's afraid, and it's okay to be afraid, but you can't let fear stop you." No, I couldn't. And I wouldn't. People could complain and harass us all they wanted; we wouldn't be stopped. Like a blanket wrapped around each sleeping child, the covering of the Lord came over us. *Thank You, Lord,* I prayed. I slept better than I had in weeks, and the next night we returned to our bedrooms.

We worked hard preparing for the start of school. We picked cotton during the day, and in the evenings we readied the children's school clothes. No one would be able to say our children weren't neat and clean. Matthew had learned to sew from his mother; at night he made underwear for the girls out of flour sacks. Help came from people we didn't even know. One day I was visiting friends down the road, and my daughter Beverly came running. "Mama," she said, "there's a white lady and a black lady waiting for you." Total strangers, they had heard about our situation. They said they were from New York and they were trying to help people like us. After taking plenty of notes and inspecting our bullet holes, they promised to tell our story and raise money from lodges, churches, synagogues, and other groups up North.

But on September 3, 1965, the first day of school, after sending my kids off on the bus, I felt alone and afraid. I lay on the bed for hours, praying, *Lord, keep my children safe.* When they finally burst through the door that afternoon I was so glad to see them again. I sat them down and made them tell me everything about their day. It hadn't been easy, but no way would they give up.

That fall I prayed every moment I could. Sometimes the children told me about being called "nigger" or having spitwads thrown at them. Once the bus driver told them to sit at the back of the bus, but they stayed up front. It broke my heart when Ruth told me one day, "I hate them. I hate those white folks."

"Ruth," I told her, "don't say that. Hate destroys you. Don't hate."

I could tell that Ruth was hurt. All fall Matthew and I continued to work in the fields, counting every penny we earned. As usual, we hoped to collect a few extra bales for ourselves by following behind the automatic picking machines. But that October, someone attached a disc to the tractor, which plowed the last of the cotton under. On December 10 the overseer told us we were ninety-seven dollars in debt, and that there was no more land for us to work. We would have to move.

Even then I couldn't hate because the covering had come back. God was with us, and I knew in spite of everything we would be all right. We would find another place to live. We would find another way to earn a living. We had stepped out in faith and God would not let us down.

We moved into Drew, where Matthew got a job. From then on all our children attended Drew High School. Seven of them eventually graduated from Ole Miss.

A lot has changed since 1965. The world's a different place. These days people tell me I showed a lot of courage back then. I have to tell them it came with the Lord's covering. That's something that never changes.

Never Forsaken

I was young and now I am old,
yet I have never seen the righteous
forsaken or their children begging bread.

PSALM 37:25 NIV

"Hello, Mother? I'm in Trouble!"

BY BEVERLY HEIRICH

Telephones always sound shrillest when they ring in the nighttime, and mine was no exception. My heart pounding, I stumbled through the 4:00 a.m. darkness of my kitchen. "Hello?" My voice was harsh with sleep.

"Hello, Mother? This is Eric. I'm in trouble."

Eric! My beautiful, intelligent, sensitive oldest child. He had celebrated his eighteenth birthday a few weeks earlier.

Instantly I was wide awake. "Are you all right?" I asked. "What's happened? What's wrong?"

"Yes, I'm fine. I just had a little accident. I need a lawyer."

"A lawyer? Why? What kind of accident?"

"I hit a motorcycle. The other guy is hurt."

"Oh, Eric. How serious is it?"

"Pretty serious..." He sounded impatient with my questions. "Can you find John Peck's home telephone number for me? I need a lawyer right away."

John Peck was my husband's corporation lawyer; Eric had met him on several occasions while visiting his father's offices.

I flipped open my directory and quickly found John's home number.

"Eric, I have the number. But please tell me, how badly is the man hurt? What hospital is he in?"

I heard my son's voice break as he uttered two words, "He's dead."

I caught my breath, speechless with horror. Dead! My child, my Eric, had killed a man!

"Mom! Hurry! They won't let me stay on the phone—what's John's number?"

Quickly I gave him the lawyer's home telephone number. Then a deeper, more mature voice cut in—a policeman. He told me Eric was under arrest for vehicular homicide. He had been drinking, driving wildly, and he had struck and instantly killed a young man on a motorcycle.

"I'll be right there," I said desperately. "Where are you? Where is Eric? I'll come immediately."

"Never mind, ma'am. We're just now in the process of booking him—he'll be transferred to another precinct within an hour or so. Just a little paperwork to get out of the way first." His voice was not unkind. "We'll be in touch with you."

He rang off quickly, and I sat alone in my darkened kitchen, trying to guess what had happened, trying to think clearly. My husband was on an extended business trip, impossible to reach until he was scheduled to call me late the next day.

John Peck! I thought. I'll see if Eric reached him. No answer when I tried the lawyer's home phone. "Good. That probably means he's on his way to help Eric."

Should I call our pastor or a friend to pray with me? No, I was reluctant to disturb anyone at that early hour. Dawn, I thought. I'll wait until dawn. Then I'll call them.

My other children continued to sleep as I sat in the quiet house, alternately praying for the dead man and his family and remembering Eric and all of our dreams for him. How proud we had always been of him. Raising him had been such a joyous adventure. And now he had killed another human being. Killed!

I thought back over the years—how we had always read Bible stories and prayed at the breakfast table; how each morning Eric was sent off to school with a kiss and a reminder to "Walk with Jesus and make someone happy."

I remembered the years of teacher conferences and the pleasure they had been because Eric was a student who had delighted his teachers with his quick mind and caring ways.

I thought of my black-lacquered jewel box. No diamonds. My rare jewels were gifts from my children. A necklace of yellow clay beads Eric had rolled and strung for me when he was eight years old—always my favorite necklace. A cameo pin, small and inexpensive—but I remembered how Eric had once walked two miles to buy it for my birthday.

I sat on in the darkness, waiting for dawn, thinking of how I had tried to nurture Eric's many gifts, striving always to help him to remember to seek God's plan for his life. How often he had heard me quote, "Give of your best to the Master; give of the strength of your youth...." And of course, every morning, "Walk with Jesus...make someone happy."

"O God!" I prayed. "I tried so hard! What more should I have done? How did I fail him?"

Looking back over the year just past, I knew when and where the signs of approaching trouble had begun. Yet all my efforts to deal with the growing problem had been frustrated.

Eric had joined the high-school wrestling team and at his coaches' suggestion—but over my objections—had begun strenuous fasting. He was naturally a slender boy, and when he fasted he turned gaunt. His personality began to change drastically. One day his sister, looking for a piece of stationery, found marijuana in his desk drawer.

When confronted, Eric became openly rebellious and ran off. We called the school, protested the fasting, told them of the marijuana—and of rumors that hard drugs, amphetamines, were being used by the wrestlers to give added energy while they fasted to make weight. The school authorities said they would look into it. They didn't call us back.

We went to the department of education, to the super-intendent of schools. Again, we were told they would investigate. Again, we heard nothing. The implied message was, "It's your problem—sad, too bad, but there's nothing we can do."

By the rime Eric graduated from high school, our family life was a shambles. We were exhausted from dealing with him and concerned about the effect he might be having on his younger brothers and sisters. He stopped seeing old friends and began to run with a wild group. More and more be seemed to be moving away from us. And now this telephone call: "Hello, Mother? This is Eric. I'm in trouble."

Dawn came at last, and as the morning light began to filter through the pale green curtains on my kitchen windows, I looked up our pastor's telephone number. When I told him what had happened, he came immediately.

As we drove through the early-morning darkness into the city to be with Eric, I cried out, "Why? What did I do wrong? I tried so hard to be a good mother—a good Christian mother! I don't understand what I did wrong. I don't understand...."

I will never forget our pastor's blunt reply. In his precise, clipped way of speaking, he said, "Listen to me, Beverly, and listen carefully. You were not a perfect mother to Eric. No child has a perfect parent. But Eric is not in police custody because he was caught doing the things you taught him to do. He is there—in jail—because he was doing the things you taught him not to do. He is in trouble because he chose to rebel against God and against his parents, just as the Prodigal Son in the Bible did. He chose to ignore and disobey the teachings of his church and home.

"So, while it's perfectly proper for you to grieve over what Eric has done, it is not proper for you to assume responsibility for his wrong choices. Eric's failure is Eric's—not yours. Perhaps this terrible experience tonight will be what turns Eric back toward home—perhaps not. But whatever happens next is not up to you, but to Eric."

As we stopped for a red light, I saw him glance over toward me with a look of profound sympathy on his face. I believe that ministers are God's representatives of Himself on earth. And as I looked at our pastor's face, so full of pain (my pain and Eric's pain, I thought), I felt a new love and a deeper appreciation for him. I knew, too, that he was trying to convey to me one of the most valuable lessons that a parent can learn: you can teach your children, but you cannot do their learning for them. What they do with what you teach them is entirely up to them. And they—not you—must bear the responsibility for their choices.

But our pastor was not finished. As the light changed and he shifted gears, he spoke again. "There's a Bible lying right there on the seat between us. Pick it up and turn to Isaiah—chapter five, verse four." His voice was gentle. "Read it out aloud, Beverly."

It took me a few minutes to find Isaiah. Then, leaning forward, I read by the small light shining from under the dashboard:

" 'What could have been done more to My vineyard, that I have not done in it? Wherefore, when I looked that it should bring forth grapes, brought it forth wild grapes?' "

As I finished reading, an enormous silence filled the car. The next thing I remember is the sound of my own sobs; I was crying softly. But the tension was gone, the heavy burden of false guilt was gone. I was no longer alone in the universe with my pain. God, my Father God, also knew what it is to have a parent's breaking heart and to ask, "Why? What more could I have done?"

The hours and days that followed were filled with pain for many people: A funeral to attend. Lawyers. Presentence investigation. A judge. Sentencing. Eventually a probation officer.

But the dark days have passed. Eric is now a college graduate and a young banker with a bright future. His brothers and sisters, his father and I, are all very proud of him.

And ever since that time, whenever I tend to think I'm all alone in my pain, that no one understands, I am brought back to reality by the memory of the voice of an almighty Father-God-Creator, crying out to the universe with the breaking heart of a parent, "What more could have been done to My vineyard, that I have not done in it? Wherefore, when I looked that it should bring forth grapes, brought it forth wild grapes?"

When I think of that, I know again that I am not alone. He understands. He understands all of it. Because He also has known what it is to suffer.

And there is not a single pathway of pain that He has not traveled. Wherever life carries me, through whatever sorrow or suffering, He has been there before me. And He reaches out His hand to say, "It's going to be all right. I've been there, and I'm here to help you through it."

Shining Promises

Our feelings do not affect God's facts.
They may blow up, like clouds, and cover the
eternal things that we do most truly believe.
We may not see the shining of the promises—
but they still shine! [His strength] is not for one
moment less because of our human weakness.

AMY CARMICHAEL

No Mere Coincidence

BY PAMELA FREEMAN

My husband and I sat at our dining-room table filling out the forms that would decide the future of our family. For two years, we'd tried to have a child. But infertility forced us to rethink our plans. We'd prayed and prayed about what to do and every sign had led us here, to this form that would officially start the process of adopting a child from Russia. Now I felt an incredible, powerful surge of confidence that we were doing the right thing. I signed the bottom and wrote the date, March 17, 2004.

That confidence carried me through the grueling months ahead. Costs for background checks, processing fees, and other requirements were high. Putting together the documents that described us, our home, our health, and our finances took months of paper-chasing, visits from a social worker, and repeated trips to government offices. Finally we completed everything and waited to hear from the adoption agency.

Then the Russian government changed its international adoption laws. What should have been a few months of waiting lasted more than a year. Had we really followed God's will? I started to wonder about the sense of confidence I'd felt the day we signed the forms.

In the spring of 2006, we got a call from the adoption agency. "There's a boy in one of our orphanages in southern Russia," the person said. "We're e-mailing you the pictures."

He was a sweet little redhead, two years old. It was love at first sight. We made our travel plans. Halfway across the world, in Volgograd, Russia, my husband and I found what we'd been praying for. The boy was shy at first, but soon he was playing and cuddling with us. I held him and didn't want to let him go.

"He has some minor medical problems," the orphanage director warned, reading through the boy's file. "We don't know who his parents were. He was abandoned when he was just a few weeks old."

I looked at my husband. Did any of that matter? He was meant for us, wasn't he? The director peered down at the boy's file again.

"He was found by a police officer," she said, "on March 17, 2004."

A Joyous Mother

He gives the barren woman a home,
making her the joyous mother of children.
Praise the LORD!

PSALM 113:9 ESV

Mama Chavez's Cocina

BY HARRIETTE CHAVEZ

Clorinda Chavez stared at me intently from her chair in the living room. She came from a New Mexican family with proud Spanish roots, and had some Old World formality about her. She'd raised seven children with her husband, Cristobal. I was about to marry their youngest, Frank. This was our first visit to his parents' house since our engagement, and I tried to hide my nervousness. In the car earlier, I'd rehearsed answers to all the things Mr. and Mrs. Chavez could possibly ask. Now my future mother-in-law leaned toward me.

"How much do you love my son?" she asked.

"I love him a whole lot," I said. "Enough to marry him."

"Do you love him enough to give me one week of your life?" she asked. "Stay with me here. I will teach you how to cook his favorite dishes, and I'll teach you about our family. Are you willing to do that before you marry my son?"

Wow. I didn't see that coming! Was this some kind of test? The few times I'd met his family, I could sense I wasn't the girl they'd imagined him bringing home. I was a Southern California girl by way of Oklahoma and Mississippi, and didn't speak a lick of Spanish. Frank wasn't bothered at all by our different backgrounds. We'd become fast friends at work. Our relationship had deepened one night at an amusement park, when the roller coaster we were riding broke down. We were stuck at the top and I was terrified...until Frank kissed me. From then on, I hadn't feared a thing with Frank at my side—except his parents. I wanted so badly for them to accept me. But living with them for a week? Was that really necessary?

"Uh...sure," I stammered. "I'd love for you to teach me to cook." But I already know how to cook—good old Southern cooking taught by my mother and grandmother. What could I learn from his mom that I couldn't from a cookbook?

A few weeks later, Frank and I drove to his parents' house again. Clorinda put Frank in his old room and set up the spare room for me.

I awoke the next morning to voices. Peaceful, poetic sounding...but way too early. I looked at the clock: 6:00 a.m. The voices came from Frank's parents' bedroom. I sat up. The walls were thin, so it wasn't hard to make out the words. Frank's father was reading a psalm. He finished and the two of them began praying for each member of their family. I heard the names of their adult children, their sons and daughters-in-law, their grandchildren. Would I soon join that prayer list? Depends how I do with the cooking, I joked to myself nervously.

I got dressed and headed to the kitchen. "Ready for your first lesson?" Clorinda asked, pouring me a cup of coffee. On the counter were some potatoes and spices. "Today we make papas fritas," she said. "Potatoes fried with onion, garlic, chili powder, and salt and pepper."

With Clorinda, it was always a dash of this, a pinch of that. She'd been making these dishes for so long, she didn't need a written recipe. It was hard to keep things straight. Still, the more we cooked, the more I learned. She showed me how to cook the best refried beans I'd ever had—a recipe passed down from her mother. She taught me how to make the tamales that were a family Christmas tradition. Next up were New Mexican "flat" enchiladas with a sauce made from dried chile pods—Frank's favorite. I was lucky to have Frank, his mother said, because he was the only male in her house who ever helped in the kitchen.

One day I bought a set of measuring cups and spoons, so I could translate Clorinda's memorized amounts. The teacup she used for dry ingredients was equal to seven-eighths of a cup. Her pinch of baking soda was one teaspoon. I was getting the hang of things...but had I won her over yet?

"Today we make tortillas," she announced one morning. Tortillas were as important as biscuits are to Southern cuisine. Mixing the dough was easy. Then she took a ball of it in her hands and rolled it out into a perfectly round tortilla. Seemed simple enough. I copied her motions...and came out with an oblong. I tried again. Even worse—this one looked like a map of the United States! I looked up sheepishly at her. Clorinda laughed. "Honey," she said, putting her arm around me, "the only way you're ever going to get round tortillas is to roll out the dough, put a saucer on top, and cut around it with a knife!" Now I laughed too. "I think you're right," I said.

By the end of the week I could make all of Frank's favorites. Clorinda even opened up about how she and Chris started their mornings. "It's important to cover your family every day with prayers," she said. "It helps you worry less about them." Now her family included me. Clorinda only expected one thing from the girl Frank brought home: that she'd be willing to continue the traditions his family held dear. And I have. I taught my children Clorinda's recipes. I've taught my daughters-in-law also. Not just her recipe for enchiladas, but for a happy marriage too.

Family Traditions

Tradition is a form of promise from parent to child. It's a way to say, "I love you," "I'm here for you," and "Some things will not change."

LYNN LUDWICK

Mom, Interrupted

BY SHERYL SMITH-RODGERS

Tomorrow was Thanksgiving, but I sure didn't feel grateful. Dragging myself around the kitchen, I pulled my chocolate-swirled cheesecake out of the oven and set it on the counter to cool. Not even its sweet aroma could get me in the holiday mood. It just made me think of my teenage son Patrick and how much he used to love digging into a thick slice. But he wouldn't be at the table at my parents' house. He didn't want to have anything to do with me.

He had been giving me the silent treatment for nearly two and a half years. He was fifteen when his father and I divorced, and he blamed me for it. The day I moved out, my daughter Lindsey came with me. Patrick didn't. He didn't even say good-bye. Whenever I called, he barely spoke. He blocked my e-mails. I invited him over for his favorite, sloppy joes—he ignored me. The only time I saw him was when I caught a glimpse of him driving his pickup truck around town, or when I dropped by the feed store where he worked. I'd hoped that he could put aside his anger for Thanksgiving—didn't he want to tease his little sister and fill up on turkey with cornbread dressing? But instead he volunteered to work at the store for his boss.

Patrick and I used to do everything together. I hadn't gone back to work after he was born. I'd strap him in a pouch on my back when I took long hikes in the woods. I pulled him around in a little red wagon until we wore out the rubber wheels. I baked for his holiday parties at school, read aloud to his class, and chaperoned their field trips. After all those years of being such a big part of my son's life, how was I supposed to be satisfied with getting tidbits about him from his sister? *Lord, I miss Patrick so much*, I prayed. *Can't You help me be his mom again?* Friends suggested buying him little gifts, or offering to take him out to dinner. I tried everything. But each attempt seemed to push him further away. Like the last time I'd seen him, a few weeks back....

That afternoon, fed up with all the ignored calls and e-mails, I'd driven to the feed store and found his pickup truck unlocked. I climbed in and waited for him to get off work. *He can't ignore me here. Maybe we can finally talk*, I thought. But when Patrick came out and saw me in the front seat, his expression turned stony.

He slid behind the wheel. "Can you get out, please?" he said. It was more a statement than a question. "Can we talk, Patrick?" I pleaded.

"I'm going to say it once more—please get out, Mother." I shook my head. "Then do me a favor and lock both doors before you leave," he snapped, sliding back out, slamming the door behind him. He climbed into a friend's car and they sped away. I sat there for a moment, shaking. Then I got out, pressed the lock button, and slowly shut the door. Why did it feel like I was closing the door on a lot more than his truck?

No wonder I don't feel thankful, I thought now, washing the cake batter from my bowls. What was it that my pastor had said last Sunday? He'd started out quoting 1 Thessalonians, "In everything give thanks." Everything?

"Instead of asking God for things you want, try thanking Him for what He's given you," he'd suggested. Okay, I thought, as I put the dishes in the rack to dry, what blessings had I overlooked in my desperation to reconnect with my son? I could be thankful for all the time I'd spent with Patrick as he was growing up. I could be thankful that he was a good kid, that he was working hard in school, that he had some close friends. I could be thankful for Lindsey and how supportive she'd been, and for the strong relationship she had with Patrick. I could be thankful that we were all healthy. There was a lot to remember. I decided to add thankfulness to my prayers.

Thanksgiving morning, before I even got out of bed, I said a prayer of gratitude. *Thank You, Lord, for another day*, I began. *Thank You for this home. Thank You for my parents. Thank You for my daughter. And thank You...thank You for my son.*

An idea nudged me. *Reach out to Patrick.* But what if he pushed me away again? *Reach out.* I sorted through a stack of greeting cards and found a blank one. "I love you more than you can ever imagine. Always," I wrote. "Happy Thanksgiving." Then Lindsey and I got ready, packed up the cheesecake, and got into the car. "I just need to make one stop," I told her.

I pulled up to the feed store and went in. There was Patrick, stacking some feed bags. He looked stressed, tired. All I wanted to do was sweep him into my arms. But I kept it low-key. "Here," I said, handing him the card. "Happy Thanksgiving!" He opened it up and read it. Was that a little smile on his face? "Tell Grandma and Grandpa hello for me," he said. I nodded and waved as I climbed back in the car. Did he just open up a little? I caught myself. *Don't get your hopes up.*

I stuck with my morning prayers of gratitude, and even thanked God for little things throughout the day. I opened up a new e-mail account and wrote Patrick chatty notes—light stuff, about Lindsey's unsociable hamster, who always hid in his cage. Or my attempt to replace the bulb in my porch light—only to discover a long rat snake coiled on top of it. I ended each with, "I love you, Mom." Was he reading them? I had no clue. But at least he wasn't blocking them.

A couple of weeks after Thanksgiving, the doorbell rang. It was Patrick. He gave me an awkward smile. "Can I come in?" he asked.

"Of course!"

I asked about school. "Goin' good," he replied. How was his girlfriend? "She's good too," Patrick said. Not much, but it was a start.

"How about coming over for some sloppy joes later this week?" I asked hesitantly.

"Can I bring a friend?" he asked.

"Sure," I said.

The dinner went pretty well. It still felt odd between us, like two people who recognized each other but didn't know from where. Then, Christmas Eve, I got the best gift ever: Patrick joined Lindsey and me at my parents' house!

Patrick started coming over for dinner every week. On his eighteenth birthday, I invited him to bring his friends too. I made sloppy joes, of course. The kids sat in the backyard around my outdoor fireplace, eating, talking, and laughing. The kind of scene I never imagined could be possible that Thanksgiving Day five months earlier.

Patrick looked over and leaned toward me. "Thank you, Mom," he said quietly. My heart soared.

Right then and there I said a silent thank-You to God. For giving me a son, and for giving me a chance to be his mother again.

A Prayer of Thanks

Thank you, Lord, for loving us unconditionally and for helping us to do the same for our children. We speak blessings upon all our children, and we thank You for sending them as blessings to us. Amen.

QUIN SHERRER

Marine Moms

BY AMBER HOWE

I was so proud when my son Dylan announced that he was joining the Marines. But now, waiting anxiously for that first call from boot camp, I could only worry. With my husband away on business, I was all alone when the call finally came. "I have arrived safely in San Diego!" Dylan recited, following the standard marine protocol. "Please do not send food or bulky items!" But underneath the scripted bravado I detected something only a mother could: a frightened boy.

Oh, God, please help him through this, I begged as I hung up. I kept seeing my son, thousands of miles away. Scared. All alone. Among strangers. And being yelled at by a drill instructor! Before I knew it, I was crying uncontrollably. I considered calling a friend, but how could anyone understand what I was feeling without experiencing it? *God, please help me through this!*

Out of nowhere, a thought popped into my head: go online.

It sounded like an order from a drill sergeant. I grabbed a tissue and headed for my laptop. I typed "Marine support group" into a search engine...and up came an organization called Marine Moms.

Like me!

"I just received my 'I have arrived' phone call and now I can't stop crying," I posted. "Help!"

By the next morning my inbox was flooded with answers. More than two hundred in all, from mothers who knew exactly how I felt.

One message in particular really hit home. "I don't know what to say to help you," said a woman named Jenny, "because my son left for boot camp today too. But I know how you feel!"

I e-mailed Jenny back right away. It turned out that her son was not only in the same company as Dylan, but in the same platoon! Jenny and I became good friends, relying on each other all through our sons' basic training, and later we even stood side by side at their graduation.

I had followed my orders and they had led me to Jenny. Our boys had made it through boot camp and were ready to serve their country. With God's help, their moms were ready too.

No Need to Fear

Do not fear, for I am with you; do not be dismayed, for I am your God. I will strengthen you and help you; I will uphold you with my righteous right hand.

ISAIAH 41:10 NIV

Hockey Mom

BY BECKY ROCHFORD

I'd hardly pulled into the driveway after work when my teenage son, CJ, flew out the front door, his lanky arms waving wildly. "We're gonna be late for practice!" he yelled. My ten-year-old, Dylan, stepped out from behind him, wearing only a long hockey jersey. "Mom, where are my hockey pants?" he called. So much for a little time to relax after work. My feet were killing me after lugging heavy equipment all day for my job at the Green Mountain Power company. But now it was time for my second (and bigger) job—mom to two busy boys.

Even the dog wanted something from me, tilting his head and whining. "Not now, Murray. You'll have to wait for your walk." I tossed Dylan the hockey pants I'd washed and folded that morning. While the boys got ready, I threw together sandwiches for them to eat in the car.

"Oh, that's another thing, Mom," CJ said. "We don't have any food." I pointed out a dozen things he could eat. "But there's no mac and cheese," he said.

"You know what?" I said, hating the sarcasm I felt creeping into my voice. "Grocery shopping takes time, and when do you think I have any time?"

Dylan appeared in the doorway. "Uh, Mom?" he said hesitantly. "I need to bring a dozen cupcakes to school tomorrow for a bake sale."

I sighed. "I'll have to do it tonight." We piled into the car. Hockey practices, overnights at friends' houses, cupcakes for school.... Did anyone care about my plans? *God, what I would give for some time for me for a change*, I thought.

Sitting in the bleachers at the hockey rink with some of the other moms, I finally had time to breathe. The puck skittered across the ice, coming to a stop against the blade of Dylan's hockey stick. With a flick of the wrist, he passed it to a teammate streaking toward the goal. Dylan's teammate took a shot. The goalie lunged but missed. Goal! I leapt from my seat. "Way to go, Dylan! Nice pass!" That looked like so much fun, zipping back and forth on the ice. When I was little, there was a pond in the woods by my family's house, and I loved to skate. But that was a long time ago. "I wish I could do that," I said to my friend Tricia, whose son had just scored on Dylan's pass.

"Really? You'd want to play hockey?"

It sounded ridiculous, sure. But at the moment, all I wanted was some fun, a break from the stress I felt. "You bet!"

"Well, if you get a team together, I'll play too," Tricia said. Was she serious? Was I? We broke out laughing. Then again, why not try? I'd like to get back on skates again. A few lessons, and maybe I could play. Was it so far-fetched?

While I stood outside the locker room waiting for Dylan to come out, I glanced at the bulletin board. "Hockey Lessons," one flyer advertised. "Call Coach Dan." I tore off a number from the bottom. *Maybe it'll be good for a laugh.*

I talked to the other moms the next day at the kids' practice. "That's a great idea," one mom said. "I've been wondering if I could do what my son does," another mom admitted. Nine moms agreed to give it a try. Enough for a team. I called Coach Dan. "I'm sorry," he replied, "but I'm all booked up."

"Wait," I pleaded. "I've got ten women ready to go!"

"Ten?" he said, curious. "Women?" He wanted to know more. Coach Dan agreed to set up four sessions.

I was excited. But what would my family think? My husband Christopher promised to take over as the family chauffeur that Saturday. And the boys? "You can borrow my skates, Mom," CJ offered. Dylan lent me his helmet. I was surprised...the boys were usually so territorial about their stuff. I'd have to buy some equipment. Fortunately, I'd spent enough time in the sporting goods store to know what to get. Hockey pants. Check. Chest protector. Check. I walked down the row of hockey sticks and pulled one from the rack. I'd bought dozens for the kids throughout the years...but this time it was for me. I was thrilled.

That weekend ten moms stepped into the rink. Well, more like wobbled. It had been a while for me, even longer for some of the others. "Line up on center ice," Coach Dan said. I moved slowly, my knees quivering. Suddenly, my legs shot out from under me. *Splat*—I fell on the ice. I wasn't the only one. Coach Dan chuckled. "Lesson one," he said, "how to stay upright."

Four sessions went by too quickly. We signed up for six more. Then eight. Stickhandling, shooting, there was a lot to learn. More moms noticed us practicing; soon there were thirty of us, enough for two teams. One day I saw another flyer on the bulletin board. Fight MS Tournament. Looking for Teams. I showed it to Coach Dan. "Think we can play?" He smiled. "Well, let me put it this way. It would be a great experience."

Our team called itself "Ray's Angels," after Tricia's uncle, who donated the entry fee and jerseys too. We chose white, black, and gold, colors of the Stanley Cup–champion Pittsburgh Penguins. Our logo was a hockey puck sprouting angel wings. And we kept practicing...hard. If I was going to play at the wing position, like my kids, I'd need to improve my shot. One afternoon, I came home and Christopher led me out to the backyard. In the center a flat, oval sheet of ice sparkled, with a hockey goal set up at one end. "For you and the boys to practice on," he said. I gave him a big hug. Dylan couldn't wait to help me work on my slap shot. We whipped pucks at the net until it was time for dinner.

Finally, game day. All the way to the rink I had butterflies. I pulled on my uniform, checked my pads, and skated out onto the ice. *This is really it.* Was this how Dylan and CJ felt before they dropped the puck? I bent my knees and got into my stance. *All right, Lord,* I thought, *maybe this is Your answer to all of my complaining.* "Go, Mom!!" I recognized that voice. I looked up. I'd sat in those stands hundreds of times. Now I was looking up at them from center ice. There were my husband and boys, cheering. "Let's go, Angels!"

It seemed like every time I touched the puck, I heard them shouting. "Yeah, Mom! Nice shot!" Not quite accolades for every dinner I made or every time I drove my kids to practice, but...in a way it was. As much as my family demanded from me, they also loved and supported me. Even in something as crazy as this.

My team didn't exactly crush our opponents that day. In fact, we lost all four games. But skating off that ice, dripping with sweat, my legs limp, I was one happy hockey mom. Pretty hard not to be when you're blessed with two boys who can't wait to hug you—sweaty jersey and all—and say, "You were awesome, Mom! Did you hear us cheering?" I couldn't have missed it.

A Good Example

We may not be able to give our children all the expensive toys, cars, computers, or cash that they want, but we sure can be good examples of what hard work and determination can accomplish.

PATRICIA LORENZ

To the Lighthouse

BY JENN GENTLESK

We were at my parents' place on the Jersey shore. It was a Sunday afternoon. My husband Anthony was watching a ballgame on TV, two-year-old Genevieve was taking a nap and four-year-old Grace was turning the pages of a book. Peace and quiet for once. The perfect time for me to get ready for the drive home. Do a load of laundry, clean up the kitchen, put the girls' stuff away, pack the car. Maybe I'd even get to that stack of papers I had to grade (I'm a high school teacher).

Then I looked out the window at the clear blue sky of a glorious September day. I should take Grace to the lighthouse, I thought. Something I'd been promising to do for months, ever since I cut out that newspaper article about the Barnegat Lighthouse's 150th anniversary: "Barnegat's guiding light to get a new shine...." That clipping was still on the bulletin board at home, half-covered with school notices and coupons. It seemed there was always something that got in the way.

I remember the first time my father took me to see Old Barney. I was five. I held his hand as we climbed the spiral staircase. I counted each and every one of the 217 steps. By the time we got to the top, both of us were breathless. Dad lifted me up so I could see over the wall. I gazed at the island stretching out in miniature far below and at the sunlight on water, sparkling as if someone had spilled a whole jar of glitter on it. I felt small and large at the same time.

I looked again at the stack of papers and the dishes in the sink, then at Grace in her sandals, pink pants and red-and-white striped shirt. I'd been telling her about the lighthouse for weeks. Now was our chance. The papers and housework could wait.

I went over to Grace. "Let's go to the lighthouse," I said.

"Just you and me, Mommy?"

"Just you and me."

"Genevieve's too young to climb the stairs, right?"

"Right."

"I think I can do it, don't you, Mommy?" she said.

"I know you can."

I grabbed my camera, and ten minutes later we were parked in the lot at Barnegat Lighthouse State Park. A half-marathon had just ended and runners were getting hugs and snapshots. Fishermen cast their lines into the inlet and couples strolled along the jetty, everyone soaking in the sunshine. I pointed out to Grace the statue of Lieutenant George Meade, who built Old Barncy in the late 1850s (and later, as a general, gained fame for defeating Robert E. Lee's forces at Gettysburg). Then the two of us entered the base of the dark, cool lighthouse.

Voices echoed above. Grace walked in front of me, holding on to the railing. The steps were painted yellow and worn from so many people walking up them. At thirty steps there was an alcove. Grace and I stopped to rest. I held her up to see the water below. "Look, a boat!" she said. She traced her finger along the glass as the boat slid out from the bay into the ocean, its wake a *V* spreading behind it.

We kept climbing. The thick brick walls blocked out all noise and I noticed that people were whispering as though we were in a church. Indeed there was something holy about this place, something peaceful and comforting in its stillness.

"Mommy, I can see the top," Grace exclaimed. She pointed to the light above and walked faster, taking me by the hand. "We're almost there!"

A minute later we were out in the bright sunshine, high above the boats in the inlet and the houses on the island. I had to catch my breath as I had many years before, but this time not only because of the long climb up to the top. The sea shimmered and sparkled in the sun, and the sky rose up from the horizon in a blanket of blue. Some places from childhood disappoint when you visit them years later. Not this one. Old Barney was just as wonderful as I had remembered, but now I was the parent here with my child.

"Look!" I said, lifting Grace up so she could see over the wall. I could feel her heart beating against mine.

"It's beautiful," she said.

"And you walked all the way up by yourself," I said.

"Mommy, take my picture!"

I set her down and she stood in front of the wall, the cerulean sky and sea behind her. I clicked a shot and then asked another visitor to take a picture of the two of us, as if I wouldn't remember this day forever, the way you hold on to these memories of what's most precious in God's world. There would be other days when I'd feel overwhelmed by work and the challenges of raising two girls, but I'd always be able to draw on this incredible blessing.

On the way down Grace asked me if I could carry her. I didn't mind. I knew that soon there would come a time when she would be too big to be carried or too independent. But right now this was our moment.

Two hundred and seventeen steps later, we were down in the parking lot. I looked back at Old Barney, standing steady above the water, its light a beacon for sailors for over 150 years, its very presence a comfort to all who gazed on it, even an overscheduled, overworked mom.

From Above

*Every good and perfect gift is from above,
coming down from the Father of the heavenly lights,
who does not change like shifting shadows.*

JAMES 1:17 NIV

A Test of Love

BY SHAR BOEREMA

H ow will he ever understand what's happening?" I said to my husband Ed that morning, staring at the documents I'd signed. This should have been a happy day for us—our son Ben's school prom. Like many eighteen-year-olds, he would soon be leaving home. For Ben, this experience, like so many in his life before, would be different.

Ed gave me a hug. "It'll be okay, honey," he said. "Ben will need time to get used to the idea." Ed looked at me closely. "So will we." But would our son ever understand our agonizing decision? Ben was a grown man physically—six-foot-two and two hundred pounds. Mentally he was three. We bathed him, dressed him, fed him, and tucked him in at night. Sometimes it was hard for me not to still see him as that dimpled-cheeked little boy I cuddled in my lap. Ben had been born severely mentally disabled, and some people tried to tell us he would be better off institutionalized. I think maybe they meant we would be better off. Ed and I were determined to raise our son at home. Along with his older sister, Jen, and younger siblings, Rachel, Aubrey, and James, we gave him a loving environment. Yes, it was hard, but never did we doubt that Ben belonged with us. I would quote my favorite Bible verse: "I have engraved you on the palms of my hands." My other children understood they were precious in God's eyes and mine. I wanted Ben to know that too. Did he? Ben uses rudimentary sign language and can only make a few sounds, like "yah!" when he's happy and "uh-uh" when he's upset. All he can write is his first initial, a crooked *B*. Yet despite communication challenges, I believed I had a deeper bond with my son. I knew what he felt and needed.

Lately, though, things hadn't been going well. Ben was changing. He acted up at school and home. He was moody and threw frightening temper tantrums. Even his siblings were wary. We heard "uh-uh" far more often than "yah!" The doctor diagnosed him with bipolar disorder, a disease that often appears in late adolescence. Now that on top of everything else. I looked back down at the papers on the table while Ed finished his coffee. We'd found a group home for severely mentally impaired adults. It was only a few blocks from the special school he currently attended. The home specialized in dealing with behavioral problems. They said they took them fishing and on camping trips. I tried to imagine Ben doing these things, tried to imagine him happy. Yes, it was the right thing to do. Yes, he needed more supervision than we could give. Yes, this was best for Ben. But nothing had broken my heart more than signing those papers to put him under the care of strangers.

That night the school auditorium was decorated lavishly for the prom. Streamers and balloons festooned the rafters, and stars glittered everywhere. I was Ben's date. His sisters had giggled and fussed over my hair and outfit, and picked out clothes for Ben (Ben's a T-shirt and jeans kind of guy). Then we posed for pictures in the backyard, Ben towering over me in his dad's sport coat, shirt, and slacks. Yet I couldn't help thinking, *He's still my little Ben*.

The lights dimmed and music filled the air. "Come on, Ben," I said, moving through the tables and chairs toward the dance floor. "I get the first dance." Around us Ben's classmates danced wildly, girls and boys flirting and having a great time. A few of Ben's friends cut in on our dance, showing off their wild moves. Ben busted a few moves himself. I gave him a thumbs-up. Ben smiled and looked me right in the eye. He seemed happy. *Lord*, I prayed, right there on the dance floor, *help me do the right thing for Ben. Guide us.*

We finished dancing and sat down for dessert. Almost immediately Ben's eyes clouded. "Uh-uh," he yelled, shaking his head. Then he pounded the table. Plates and silverware jumped. Everyone looked up, startled. He began to bring his fist down again but I grabbed his arm. "No, Ben," I said. "Look at the cake. It looks good, right? You love cake." It was touch-and-go. He was agitated, and I knew he was on the verge of a bipolar episode. I thought one more dance would help, but no. We had to leave early.

The next day Ed and I sat with Ben at the kitchen table while he drew faces on paper. "Ben, you're going to have a new house,"

I said. "But we will come see you all the time. Can you draw a house, Ben?"

"Uh-uh," he said, raising both hands. Over the next weeks I took every opportunity to tell Ben about his new home. We drove past it after school several times. I made a drawing for him. "You'll sleep in another house," I said. Ben didn't understand. Or maybe, I feared, he just couldn't accept it.

One morning we drove Ben over to the home to move some of his things in, hoping it might get him used to the idea. The staff gave us a tour. Ben's eyes grew wide at the big-screen TV in the TV room. He checked out his new bedroom and seemed to approve, especially when we put a TV on his dresser with some of his favorite videos. Then we began to bring his things in, his clothes and a poster of *The Lion King* that had hung on his wall at home. Finally Ben helped us lift his favorite chair from the back of the van, an old cozy recliner that we moved into his room right by the window. He looked confused but didn't act out. *He still doesn't understand*, I thought, as we drove home. *Lord, what will happen when we really leave him?*

I was sitting at my desk the next day still thinking about this when Ben poked his head in. "Yes, Ben?" He came and stood in front of me, all six-foot-two, but still my little boy. Slowly he brought his hands together to form a roof. "Huss?" he asked.

Tears filled my eyes and a verse filled my heart. *I have engraved you on the palms of my hands....* "Come here, Ben," I said, my voice breaking. "When you go to your new house, I want you to remember how much Mama loves you." I held him tight until he gently pulled away. He reached over and took a pen from my desk. Then he opened my hand. He touched the tip to my palm and carefully drew the one thing he knew—that crooked but unmistakable *B*.

Written on His Palms

What matters supremely is not the fact that I know God, but the larger fact which underlies it—the fact that He knows me. I am graven on the palms of His hands. I am never out of His mind. All my knowledge of Him depends on His sustained initiative in knowing me. I know Him because He first knew me.

J. I. PACKER

Homeless Babies and Babyless Homes

BY MARY PICKFORD

Have girl for adoption along lines discussed," the telegram read. Perhaps the most thrilling message in my life—it was from an orphanage.

Buddy and I were on a plane the next morning, excited at the thought that our search might be over. But I personally had a feeling of panic too. We had been years trying to find a child. Once before we had settled on an adorable two-week-old baby girl. All formalities and paper-signing had been completed, and we had even prepared a nursery for the baby in our home. A day or so before the child was due to arrive—she died.

Since then I had often wondered, although I battled such thoughts, if God really wanted me to have a child. It had seemed like a double deprivation to have to close the door on that empty nursery. And yet why had God given me such an insistent urge for children—and an almost obsessed love for babies? My idea of the perfect home had always been four children—and it still is.

At the orphanage we learned somewhat to our dismay that the girl in question was eight years old. We had asked for a baby.

"Does the child know we have come to see her?" I asked the woman in charge.

She shook her head. "We never build up the hopes of any child by giving advance notice."

I looked around for my husband, but he had stepped out the door to the playground, evidently attracted by the shouts of some boys playing ball. Moving over to the window, I too watched the action. One small lad with tousled hair and quick, agile movements interested me at once. He seemed to run the hardest and throw a ball the straightest. Although the smallest boy on the field, he by his eagerness and ability was the recognized leader.

Buddy too, I could see, was engrossed in this youngster. As soon as the matron of the home returned with the girl, I asked her about the lad. "We would be glad to have you meet him, Mrs. Rogers," she told me.

Buddy and I had already talked with the girl when the boy was brought in and introduced. He marched straight up to us, shook hands firmly, looking us both in the eye. There was much wisdom in that six-year-old look. I was sure that Buddy had the same feeling about him that I did, but I relied upon a little double talk in front of the boy to check my husband's reactions.

"We ought to make some decision about closing the deal," I said.

"I'm all for it, but remember, dear, it's a long-term investment," he replied.

"I know, but the best one we'll ever make." And we smiled our joint decision.

We called our boy Ronny Rogers.

Every couple who considers adoption has some fear as to how it will work out. An infant probably absorbs an atmosphere. The older the child, people feel, the more adjustments will have to be made. These and other thoughts were in my mind as we left the orphanage that day with Ronny. Yet one unmistakable fact loomed far above any other. We had gone into the orphanage man and wife—and had come out a family.

Once in our home Ronny belonged as if he had been there all his life. True, a small boy is at some disadvantage when he transfers from an orphanage environment to a large Hollywood home where he is in somewhat of a spotlight. Yet no child has been more loved than Ronny, and he has known this from the start. This love is all that really matters to a child whether his parents live in a two-room flat, a mansion, or a house by the side of the road.

There are thousands of youngsters in institutions and foster homes who are well fed and well taken care of. What they do not have—something more important almost than being well fed— is the sense of belonging, of being loved. My heart aches for these children. But it also aches for all the homes without children; for the couples who deprive themselves of the one thing it takes to make a home and a family—children to love.

I had asked for a girl and expected an infant. If I had any disappointment at finding myself with a six-year-old boy, it didn't last long. Ronny completely assaulted our hearts. I thank God for so guiding us. Almost everyone wants an infant, but those from six to fourteen years of age are the ones really in need of a home. So much happiness flooded our house with the arrival of Ronny that we soon decided to enlarge the family some more.

Within ten months the Lord sent me what my heart fancied—an infant baby. Please don't be skeptical when I use the phrase "the Lord sent me," because when I think of the years I had been searching for an infant to adopt...the delays, the heartbreak, the difficulties and involvements that go with adoption, you can understand why I truly felt that God meant this particular child for me.

We named the baby Roxanne and everyone in the house was completely happy—except Ronny! "She's a nuisance," he had said. "What's so wonderful about her? Just another girl."

But Ronny too was slowly to succumb to Roxanne's baby charms. We watched the air of brother-ownership and self-appointed censor and guardian develop.

No home can be a completely happy one without God. Bible reading and prayer have been to me like the foundation of a building. With sound religious training as a basis, children can grow up to become better citizens, and I find parents themselves acquire new depth and understanding while teaching the importance of God's teachings to their offspring.

Roxanne's childish faith is especially appealing. The moment she overhears any discussion about God, whether it be in a small family gathering, or a room full of people, she interrupts with her pet phrase: "There iz no spot where God iz not."

I think my deepest satisfaction came one day when Ronny and I and a cousin were driving to see the newborn baby of my niece.

"Just think," said my cousin who was driving and forgot for the moment, I suppose, that Ronny was in the back seat, "how wonderful to have a child of your own flesh and blood."

I grew cold with horror for a moment, thinking of how Ronny would feel, and I said as casually as I could: "Yes, wonderful—but it's a little terrifying wondering how they're going to turn out."

From the back Ronnie spoke up instantly: "Just think how lucky you were, Mother! I was six years old and you could tell exactly what you were getting."

I laughed back at him, thankful that his eyes glowed with pride and importance. No sense there of not belonging; he knew he was wanted. And I was warmed inside with fresh love for my family and gratitude to God for the fulfillment of a lifelong dream—a home with children.

A Beautiful Plan

God has a wonderful plan for each person He has chosen. He knew even before He created this world what beauty He would bring forth from our lives.

LOUISE B. WYLY

The Mother I Had Always Known

BY BARBARA WERNECKE DURKIN

I'd always welcomed the friendly sound of my brother's voice calling from Maryland, but this time his words jolted me as I stood with the kitchen phone to my ear. "Bar," said Dick somberly, "we have to make a decision tonight. The nursing home we found down here can only hold a place for Mom until the morning, and she'll have to be in the room within a few days. They want to know right away. Call me back in an hour."

After I hung up I stared at the phone for a long time before moving. One hour. One hour to decide whether to send our Alzheimer's-stricken mother from upstate New York all the way down to southern Maryland, where I wouldn't be able to see her regularly, couldn't supervise her care or oversee her daily routine.

One hour versus three years. That's how long my husband Bill and I would have to wait to get Mom into an acceptable facility near us. We were not sure we could handle another three years of caring for Mom. Now Dick and his wife had found a good home that could take Mom immediately.

I went into the living room and told Bill. We talked together quietly and agreed: Dick's plan was best for Mom. We'd known all along it might come to this.

The crushing prospect of being separated from Mom now that she needed me most tormented me. We'd always been a great team, Mom and I. Dad died when I was a teenager, and Mom raised me on her own. We'd braved many tough times together. Mom showed me how to face life's worst moments with courage, grit, and—most of all—good humor. She always laughed her way through hard jobs and sang through bad days. "Everyone is my friend," she'd say, and because she believed it, it was true. My mother had always been there for me, giving me strength when I needed it most.

But Mom had not really been there for me in recent years. I was the one who was giving strength now.

Except for increasingly rare moments of lucidity, she'd become lost in her own private world of memory and fantasy. Television no longer interested her because she couldn't follow the plots. Reading was hopeless for the same reason. Once we would sit for hours laughing and gossiping; now after a few sentences her interest would wane and she'd fix her gaze on some distant spot in some distant twilight world I was not a part of. I was powerless against the thief that was stealing her mind.

"Where are we now?" she'd demand as she sat gazing out our dining room window at the birds. "Whose house is this, anyway?" Mom could be difficult and stubborn, even irrational. Sometimes she was impossible. The strain wore me down day by day. After listening to her sing the same repetitious song or poem, perhaps a hundred times in one afternoon, my nerves were shot by the time Bill and the boys got home. Everyone was affected.

At night, though, when I tucked her into bed, Mom would invariably remember to say her prayers. Like a little child she would recite the old familiar "Now I lay me down to sleep," the first prayer she taught me when I was a girl. Then she would bless her sisters and all of us, because she did, indeed, still know who we were and how she was connected to us. That was the one foundation her sickness couldn't erode.

I too would say my prayers at bedtime, asking God to give me strength to help Mom. But I was helpless to halt Mom's deterioration. Each day her lustrous emerald eyes grew more muddied. I wondered how long it would be before they looked at me blankly and saw only a stranger.

There were two days of sorting, packing, and complicated paperwork before we left for Maryland. They were the saddest days of my life, a life that had been spent never very far from my mother. "Who'll make sure she has everything she needs?" I worried aloud to Bill. I asked God to give me more strength, but I didn't feel it. I knew that Mom required professional supervision, yet the thought of a stranger coming to her in the night, when she would ramble and wander around like a sleepwalking child, seared me with guilt.

I packed what I thought Mom would need in her tiny half-room at the home. The trip down was a blur. In my mind I kept trying to slow time, to stretch out these final hours before I faced what I wasn't sure I could handle. But everything seemed to be moving so fast.

Before I knew it I was signing the documents at the nursing home, while Mom looked on with a sort of dull curiosity. It was an excellent, well-staffed nursing home where Mom would get the best of care, but she didn't really seem to grasp what was happening. I took her arm and we walked her to the room marked 107-A. There was a bed with Mom's name over it. Mom was dressed in her usual slacks and colorful top and her favorite shoes, red high-top Reeboks. She sat on the narrow bed swinging her feet like a little kid.

Dick and Marge left quickly—they'd look in on Mom daily. Bill and the boys kissed her and headed for the parking lot. They promised we'd be back to visit. But I couldn't bring myself to say good-bye. I kept asking her every foolish little question that popped into my head: Did she remember where the bathroom was? Did she remember her roommate's name? Did she know where I put her hairbrush and mirror? All sorts of silly things.

Finally there was nothing more to ask or say. I stared at Mom, sitting on her new bed. I wondered if she completely understood what was happening or what I was feeling. Then I wrapped my arms around her. I held on for dear life. I hugged and hugged and kissed and kissed her. I stained her bright sweater with angry tears. *Why does it have to end like this, God?* I demanded. These were supposed to be the golden years for Mom, years when I could make her happy. I'd always planned the best for Mom in her old age. Now I was saying good-bye.

Abruptly she pulled away. There was a sudden spark in her eyes, a piercing look of recognition and the old fire. She sat up straight and tall. "Stop crying now," she said firmly. "Say good-bye and get going. Don't worry about me. Everyone here is my friend. I will be well taken care of."

She looked hard at me for about five seconds as I stood still with amazement and stared into the face of the mother I had always known, that familiar mom who knew and understood, who laughed and sang and was strong for me when I needed her. "Mom!" I cried, and reached out for her. But it was like reaching for a phantom. As quickly as my "real" mom had appeared, she dissolved again into the little child swinging her feet in their bright red sneakers.

My mother let go of me when I could not let go of her. For one last brave time she was strong for me. And for a moment God showed me His love in a small miracle I knew was a sign that He would watch over Mom now that I no longer could, the way He watches over mothers everywhere.

Safe and Secure

The eternal God is your refuge, and underneath are the everlasting arms.

DEUTERONOMY 33:27 NIV

Never Far Away

BY CAROL L. MACKAY

When the girls were young I could hear them calling for me at night, "Mom, Mom!" if they were sick or troubled, and I would go rushing down the hall to their bedsides. But this time when I heard the cry "Mom, Mom!" both daughters were grown, and Kathryn was a married woman, traveling halfway around the world with her husband Peter. Still, it was unmistakable: she was calling me.

Picking up a Bible from the nightstand, I went into the family room to pray. I had a feeling of great urgency; Kathy needed help. "Dear God, show me what to do, I prayed. Then I turned to the 91st Psalm, repeating it over and over again, before I was able to feel at peace.

A few weeks later we got a letter postmarked from Singapore. "I'm grateful to be able to write this," Kathy began. "I can now tell you I was quite ill in Borneo with some sort of flu. We were there, doing our usual exploring one afternoon, when I suddenly became very sick and feverish.

"Back in our room, Peter became worried. As I rambled incoherently, he searched for someone who knew of a good doctor. Finally he found a local doctor who came to our scruffy, rented room. Seeing our predicament, this good man invited us to his house, where he and his housekeeper nursed me back to health—thank God."

What touched me most came at the end of the letter. "Remember when I was a girl, and I would call out, 'Mom,' and you would come rushing down the hall? That night in Borneo, in my fever, I called...

"And then I could hear you rushing down the hall."

Always There

It's so good to know that wherever you are, your mom is with you in spirit and in love.

UNKNOWN

The Perfect Card

BY MAVIS CHAPLIN

On the way home from work that Friday I entered a greeting card store and joined a large crowd milling around the Mother's Day section. The woman next to me smiled ruefully. "I guess a lot of us are just so busy that we put this off," she said.

I nodded wearily. In previous years my sister had always taken on the chore—in my eyes, it was a chore—of purchasing a Mother's Day card. Then she'd sign both our names to it. My mother and I had never had the best relationship, and it had always been a relief to me that Karen had taken care of the card. But Karen had married six months earlier and wanted to buy Mom her own card, from herself and her husband.

"So you're on your own this year," she'd said.

That I was. I sighed and picked up a card at random. As I read the words, my lips pressed together tightly. MOM, YOU'RE SO UNDERSTANDING. I shoved that card back into the slot. Understanding? Like the time I told her I wanted to drop out of college? She screamed at me and threatened to throw me out of the house if I did.

I tried a second that said, MOM, I COULD ALWAYS TALK TO YOU! Back it went, fast. I thought of the time I brought home the boy I was in love with. As soon as the door shut behind him, she told me she'd disown me if I ever got serious with him. "He'd be nothing but trouble," she said. When I started to defend him, she just walked away.

I reached for another card. MOM, YOU WERE ALWAYS THERE FOR ME! This one had a charming drawing of a girl and her mother smiling radiantly at each other across a kitchen table. My stomach tightened. Well, that's sure not my mother and I. With her demanding secretarial job and chronically unemployed husband, and problems with her own ailing mother, Mother was too preoccupied to pay attention to me. When I tried to talk to her about boys or girlfriends or problems with teachers, she brushed me off.

Many times, I'd asked God to help rid me of my bitterness. But now it flared up again. I eyed a card that blared in large type: TO A PERFECT MOTHER. I left the store without a card. Maybe Mom wouldn't notice if I didn't give her one.

The next day, I went for an early morning bike ride with my friend Sandy. Over tall iced-coffees after our ride, Sandy asked, "What did you get your mom?"

"Not even a card," I admitted. At her wide-eyed stare, I hastened to justify myself. "Do you ever," I asked, "feel that your mother didn't do a very good job as a mother?"

"What an awful thing to say!" she told me. "My mother passed away when I was six. And if I had a mother now, I would never, ever say anything like that about her! You should feel grateful you have a mother."

Humiliated, I stared into my glass. A few minutes later, I made an excuse to go, saying I'd remembered some work I had to do at my office.

Once I'd said that, I felt I had to make it true, so I headed for the city. Maybe going to work would take my mind off the card problem.

I was wrong. In the office I put my head down on my desk.

After a moment, I heard a tentative, quiet hello. It was my boss, Jenna. "Are you all right?" she asked.

I guess I needed to pour out all my feelings. Twenty minutes later I said, "...and so maybe I just won't get her any card at all!" I stopped, aghast at what I'd just confided.

Jenna was thoughtful. "You know," she said slowly, "it's only natural to have mixed feelings about people we're close to. Husbands. Kids. Even mothers. We have such high expectations of our mothers, they're bound to let us down sometimes."

Sometimes? "What do you think I should do about the card?" I asked.

She looked straight at me. "Whenever I'm having a problem, I ask God for help."

I stared at her. "You think I should ask God for help in picking out a greeting card?" I would have rolled my eyes, but I didn't want to offend my boss.

"Exactly. Just ask God for His help and then go to a card store. God will put the right card into your hand."

Oh, sure, I thought. Boss or no, I said, "I'm sure God has far more important things to do with His time!"

Her brown eyes met mine. "What could be more important than healing a relationship between a mother and daughter? And if you didn't love your mother, you wouldn't be so torn."

"You're the boss," I said finally.

As I rode alone down in the elevator, my prayer was more like a challenge. "Okay, God. Show me just the card I need!" I felt foolish pestering Him with this petty request.

When I got to the store, I felt even more foolish. The Mother's Day card rack was almost empty! There were about thirty cards left, looking picked over and worn. I gave a mental shrug.

I pulled one out and flipped it open. I felt more hopeless than ever as I read the message. It had the typical gushy sentiment inside: "You are always a treasure to me. I'm so glad we're related...." Maybe, I thought, some of Jenna's faith has rubbed off on me. Otherwise, why would I be feeling such disappointment? I sighed and closed the card.

That's when I noticed the writing on the cover. In gold print, it read: TO MY DAUGHTER ON MOTHER'S DAY.

To my daughter? For a minute I didn't understand, and then I realized this was a card someone had stuck in the wrong section.

Suddenly I pictured my mother at a card rack, trying to choose a card for me. What would that experience be like? Every birthday she sent me a card—something like To My WONDERFUL DAUGHTER. Well, surely I was not as wonderful as those cards suggested. If I matched myself against any of the "perfect daughter" cards, might I not come up lacking too?

I mentally replayed some of those old scenes I had so resented, only this time from a different angle. I thought of my mother working long hours at her job so that she could give me a good education. And then I saw myself coming home after the first term in college, breezily announcing, "I'm going to quit school." My mother, who'd always wanted to go to college, had never been able to afford it. And there I was, casually about to throw away something she had struggled to make possible for me. Because of Mom I hadn't quit; I had completed college. I remembered her pride when she took snapshot after snapshot of me in my cap and gown.

Another scene: Mother, wanting me to have an easier life than she had had, carefully scrutinizing my boyfriends. She wanted to make sure I found one who would help provide a secure and loving future for me, unlike my father, who had provided neither for her. No wonder she thought that boyfriend was not right for me—and hadn't I myself soon realized it? I remembered how Mom had beamed when I introduced her to my husband-to-be.

Could my mother ever send me a card saying To My PERFECT DAUGHTER? Hardly! And yet, judging by all the flowery cards she'd sent over the years, despite our numerous differences, my mother loved me.

Jenna had said if I prayed, God would put the perfect card in my hand. And He had. Only not in the way I'd expected. Now I made my way over to a different section. BLANK CARDS said the description on the silver banner above the racks. WRITE YOUR OWN MESSAGE. I'd send my mother a beautiful card with a bouquet of flowers on the front. Inside would be the perfect message, for it would be in my own words, just the way I felt them:

"To my mother on Mother's Day—Thank you for being you! With love from your (imperfect) daughter."

A Good Mother

There is no way to be a perfect mother, and a million ways to be a good one.

JILL CHURCHILL

A Song for Mom

BY EDWARD GRINNAN

S tupidly I'd lost a credit card and was on the phone trying to get a new one rushed to me. The customer-service rep, whom I suspected was not currently in the same hemisphere as me, took my info then asked in a lilting accent a secret security question: "What is your mother's birthday?" I hadn't remembered ever having divulged this, and I am bad at dates in any case, but this one I knew.

It was just the two of us one year. I was about ten and obsessed with the trombone. Dad was stuck on a business trip and my brother and sister were now both away at college. Mom and I ate dinner in the kitchen. She brought out a little cake with a single candle and we sang a halfhearted "Happy Birthday." Mom, who lacked my sweet tooth, took a tiny piece, and I devoured the rest then tore back upstairs to my trombone and my scales. A few minutes later I came back down for something when I stopped and noticed my mom, alone, standing at the sink doing our meager dishes. I'd never felt sorry for my mom before because she never felt sorry for herself. Yet here it was her birthday and all she had was me and a sink full of dishes. I tiptoed upstairs, grabbed my trombone, then marched into the kitchen playing the most awful, off-key version of "Happy Birthday" you can imagine. Mom stood with her back to me until I was mercifully through, then turned. There were tears in her eyes, a rare sight. She walked over and with her sudsy hands hugged me as hard as she ever had or ever would.

"September 20," I told the woman on the phone.

"Thank you," she said from the other side of the earth. "It's nice when a man knows his mother's birthday."

Yes, mothers make the world go 'round.

Mom's Purpose

I thought my mom's whole purpose was to be my mom. That's how she made me feel.

NATASHA GREGSON WAGNER

"Please Save My Babies"

BY MONICA SOTO

A n uneasy feeling crept through me after I picked up the telephone that evening. The caller, a man, asked for a person whose name I did not recognize. "Sorry, you have the wrong number," I said, and hung up. But I kept thinking of the voice on the phone. I knew that voice. It had to be Fernando, an ex-boyfriend I hadn't seen for more than three years.

I had met Fernando in 1993 after I came to the United States as a fifteen-year-old with my mother from Costa Rica. He seemed a nice-enough young man, but after we started dating, he became insanely jealous. He would not allow me to say hello to any other boy. It got so bad that when friends passing by called, "Hi, Monica. How are you?" he wouldn't let me reply. He also drank a lot, which seemed to intensify his jealousy.

By then I had dedicated my life to Christ, and I knew that kind of jealousy was not only unnatural but a sin. After much prayer, I finally told Fernando I could not live like that and it would be best for us to separate.

His face darkened and he vowed, "One day I am going to get you back." I felt sorry for him, but I knew it was best.

A year later I met Juan. We attended the same church, and his gentle smile touched me. He was so kind and thoughtful. We fell in love and were married. Our daughter, Jacqueline, was born a year later. Juan, who was from Guatemala, worked very hard. First he was in landscaping and then got a good job in construction. Mom, Dad, and my little brother and sister lived in an apartment in Spring Valley. Juan and I joined them since we couldn't afford our own place. Mom and Dad both worked to help pay bills, and I took care of my baby and the house and did the cooking.

We had cause for celebration a year later when I became pregnant again. Later, the doctors told me I was carrying twin boys. Juan was so thrilled.

"God is so good to us," he said. I knew he had been hoping for a son. Now he would have two.

Naturally, I had no contact with Fernando. Once, however, I heard through others that he was living with some men in New Jersey and was drinking heavily. I felt sorry for him and prayed he would find the Lord as Juan and I had.

But now that strange "wrong number" phone call—was it really him? Then, knowing I couldn't worry about it, I put it out of my mind.

I was feeling good that Wednesday in October. It was a beautiful fall afternoon. I was preparing my family's supper.

Jacqueline was asleep in a bedroom and my twin boys were showing signs of life in my expanding body. I smiled as I stirred the beans; in two months my husband and I would be holding our babies in our arms.

As I glanced at the kitchen clock, which showed 3:00 p.m., I heard a sound—as if someone were trying to open our front door. I knew it was locked. Could it be my nine-year-old sister Maria coming home from school? Her bus was due soon, but I hadn't heard its noisy approach. I looked out, but no one was there. I turned back to my cooking, using a towel to wipe perspiration from my brow. It was getting warm in the kitchen because of the oven, so I decided to open the patio doors for fresh air.

As I was checking the oven I heard a step behind me. I turned, looked up, and gasped. It was Fernando! He looked strange and held his hands behind him.

"What are you doing here?" I cried. I grabbed the kitchen phone to dial 911, trying to keep it out of his sight, but I couldn't hit the right buttons, I was so shaken. Fernando's voice was grim. "I'm sorry, Monica, but you have destroyed my life."

"What do you have in your hands?" I choked.

He brought his hand around and aimed a pistol at me.

I screamed. "No! What are you trying to do? You cannot do that. I am pregnant. If you are going to kill me, please wait until I have my babies," I begged.

Oh, God, I implored silently, *please save my babies.*

"Sorry," he repeated, "but you destroyed my life."

I heard my sister's school bus groan to a stop outside. "Fernando," I choked, "my sister is coming."

"I don't care about that!" he snarled, and as he said it the pistol muzzle flared and there was a deafening explosion. Something like a sledgehammer slammed my chest and my legs melted under me, as if my lower body were floating in water.

I found myself lying on the floor looking up at Fernando. In horror I saw him press the gun to his head and pull the trigger. I screamed hysterically as he crashed onto the floor.

I heard Maria outside crying and I called, "Maria, go through the patio." I was so frightened, not knowing if Fernando was alive or dead. When Maria ran into the kitchen, her eyes were wide with terror.

God, I believe, gave Maria presence of mind. That little child picked up the telephone and dialed 911. As I lay moaning, I could hear her talking to the dispatcher. "My sister has been shot." She gave our address and explained that I was pregnant with twins. Then she turned to me, relaying the dispatcher's questions about where I had been hurt. She told them about Fernando lying on the floor. She was so calm and reasoned.

In minutes sirens were screaming outside the apartment. Soon some men placed me on a stretcher and put me in an ambulance. As we raced to Nyack Hospital, I kept praying for my babies. Despite being in agonizing pain, the thought of them was what kept me conscious. Juan was waiting at the hospital. He hugged me and I asked, "Fernando?"

"He's dead," said Juan.

In surgery they found the bullet had torn through my heart and lodged in my spine. That was why I couldn't feel my legs. I had lost 70 percent of my blood. When they placed the mask on my face before operating on my heart, I slipped into unconsciousness, still pleading with God to save my twins. When I awoke, nurses and doctors clustered around me. All I could ask was, "My babies? My babies?"

A nurse put her hand on my shoulder and nodded. "They are all right."

"Oh, thank You, God," I cried, tears of relief streaming down my face.

The doctor said they had successfully repaired my heart and they would birth my sons by Cesarean section. Then he grew solemn and took my hand. "Monica, I must tell you, because of the bullet in your spine, you will never walk again."

I looked him straight in the eyes. "You may think that, doctor, but I do not, for I believe with God's help, I will walk again."

Two days later our two sons, Kenneth Daniel and Juan Carlos, were born, each weighing less than three pounds. Being premature, they had to be placed in incubators. But soon Juan and I got to hold them. They were gifts from God and together we thanked Him.

Have I forgiven Fernando? Of course; God says we must forgive those who have hurt us, just as He forgives us. I believe Fernando was not in his right mind when he did that terrible thing.

Two months after that, both babies were at home with me, doing well and growing. Kenneth was twelve pounds and Juan ten. At night when they made it clear they were hungry, my husband was the one who got up, but he brought them to me so I could bottle-feed them. I can do just about everything for them from a wheelchair—change their diapers, clothe and bathe them.

As I hold my sons and sing lullabies to them, their brown eyes look up at me so trustingly, and it is as if God is telling me not to worry about the future. So I look forward to it. Already He is providing. My mother now stays home to take care of my three babies when I go to daily therapy.

A fund drive by local people has helped a lot with expenses. "I feel a little guilty," says Juan. "We did not come here to America to take from others." So Juan is planning to get a part-time night job.

We know much work lies ahead. We have dreams of our three children going to college and contributing to this wonderful country that means so much to us.

And my own special dream? Both Juan and I believe I will walk again. In a way, we think it is good that the doctors have put themselves on record saying I won't. For when I am fully healed, no one can say, "Oh, that doctor made Monica well." In this way, Jesus will surely get the glory.

Answered Prayer

Hear my cry, O God
listen to my prayer;
from the end of the earth I call to you
when my heart is faint.
Lead me to the rock
that is higher than I,
for you have been...
a strong tower against the enemy....
Let me take refuge under the shelter of your wings!

PSALM 61:1–4 ESV

Spring Break?

BY DAWN MEEHAN

I t was the third day of spring break. A break for my kids, not me. I am a stay-at-home mom of six kids (seven, if you count my husband Joe), and they wanted to let me know what a good time they were having—as early in the morning and as loudly as possible. Who needs an alarm clock when you have fourteen-year-old Austin and ten-year-old Jackson tearing through the house yelling at the top of their lungs (the only volume at which a kid can yell inside the house) and whipping pillows at each other first thing in the a.m.? Good morning!

Our television had been broken for three weeks. The part we needed to fix it was apparently being delivered by water buffalo. Joe's car was in the shop. "You don't mind if I take the van, do you?" he'd said the night before. No, of course not. Being cooped up in the house with six kids and no TV to occupy them has always been my idea of fun. I got out of bed, dreading what the day might bring. At least the weather was warm—46 degrees, which almost qualified as tropical here in Chicago in April. I'd been praying for days for the snow to melt so I could send the kids outside to play and burn off some energy. I walked into the kitchen, spilled cereal crunching underfoot, and made myself a cup of coffee. "Can we go outside and play?" my three youngest asked.

"Sure," I said, opening the kitchen door and releasing them. Well, even if the sky said Antarctica, the calendar said it was spring. Another cup of coffee and I might be brave enough to help Savannah, twelve, my oldest daughter, tackle the mess in her bedroom.

Savannah likes her room nice and neat. She shares a room with Lexi, seven, who prefers disarray. "Don't worry, Savannah," I said. "I'll help you shovel a path to your bed." We unearthed Barbie dolls, Barbie dresses, Barbie's car and washing machine, a headless Barbie (Clayton's handiwork?), Community Chest cards from Monopoly (oh, that's where those went), wrapping paper from a birthday party two months before, and a hard brown object that looked suspiciously like a petrified hot dog. It was an archaeological dig with the oldest stuff at the bottom. Savannah burrowed under a crumpled Snow White costume and emerged triumphant. "My hair brush!"

Then Jackson walked into the room carrying a snow shovel. "Look what I found," he said. Lying there motionless at the end of the shovel was an opossum. It looked dead or maybe it was just playing possum...how could you tell the difference? I wasn't about to find out.

"Jackson," I said in a calm and collected voice, "WHAT ARE YOU DOING?! Why would you scoop up a wild animal and bring it into the house? Use your brain, boy!" He turned and the shovel tipped precariously. Great, the possibly deceased opossum was going to fall on the floor. "Take that back outside this minute," I ordered. "And leave it outside." Just in case he got any different ideas. (What is it with boys and critters, anyway?)

I finished up in the girls' room and headed back to the kitchen with a big bag of garbage. I stopped in my tracks. The floor was covered in muddy footprints. I'd prayed for the snow to melt. Here was my answer.

Where were the paper towels? I looked at the counter. There were breadcrumbs, open jars of peanut butter and jelly, and bowls, spoons, whisks, and measuring cups where Savannah had mixed up a pan of extra-gooey brownies. I think it's great that my kids can cook. Someday they will learn to clean up too.

All I could find were the diaper wipes. I used those to scrub the mud off the floor. Brooklyn, my three-year-old, wandered in from the yard.

"Where's your coat?" I asked her.

"Outside," she answered. "I don't need it. It's hot."

"And your shoes?"

"Outside."

"It's forty-six degrees. Practically swimming weather."

"I go swimming!" Brooklyn said excitedly. Not until she got her diaper changed. And I had the wipe right in my hand. I went out to throw the dirty diaper away—only to discover the kids had taken their food outside for a picnic. In the mud.

ZZZ, the dryer made the pleasant noise it does when a load is finished. I dashed in to take the clothes out. Shirts, pants, socks, sweats (somewhere between baby number three and baby number four I stopped sorting laundry). There was a new color on everything. Dabs of brilliant purple. I scratched at it and it stuck to my hand. Ah, gum. Gum on socks and pants and sweatshirts. "Who left gum in their pocket?" I shouted, even though I knew who the culprits were: I Dunno and Not Me.

Brooklyn came trotting out in her bathing suit. Let's see. Muddy footprints crisscrossing the kitchen floor. Check. Gum stuck to a dozen articles of just-laundered clothing. Check. Dishes piled up to the ceiling. Check. Baby wearing a bathing suit in 46-degree weather. Check. Opossum on a shovel. Check. A typical day at our house, never mind the added bedlam of spring break.

Lexi darted past wailing, "Mom, Jackson hit me." Jackson, hot on her trail, retorted, "Yeah, well, she shot a Nerf dart at my ear."

"It was an accident." "Was not!" "Was too!" "Was not!" "Was too!"

I looked at the clock. Only four days, eighteen hours, and twenty-three minutes until they went back to school. And more important, only one more hour until my husband would get home from work, at which point I would tender my resignation and board a plane for Bora Bora. I don't know where Bora Bora is, but I bet they don't have opossums there.

An hour later Joe got home and asked, "So what did you do all day?"

I locked myself in our bedroom to pray for serenity. I mean, fold some laundry. I didn't want to be a mother anymore. What was I doing this for? I was tired of settling arguments, cleaning floors, chasing down orphan socks, coaxing a three-year-old out of her bathing suit into warmer clothes. God would have to find some other profession for me. Lion tamer would be fine. In fact, lion tamer wasn't so far from what I was doing already.

I heard a small scratching sound in the hallway. I looked over at the door and saw a folded piece of paper being slipped under it. What now? I went over and picked the paper up. I unfolded it. There was a crayon drawing of the eight of us holding hands and smiling. "I love you, Mommy," was written on the bottom. "You're the best Mommy in the world. Love, Lexi."

A smile tugged at the corners of my mouth and the stress of the day began to melt away. I gazed at the drawing and thought about the kids' impromptu picnic in the mud. Okay, even I'd said 46 degrees was balmy for April in Chicago. I recalled the brownies Savannah made. I've taught my kids to cook and they like it—I must be doing something right. Then I pictured the opossum on the shovel and that just cracked me up. What did I need TV for? I was part of the most amazing reality show on earth!

All at once I heard giggling coming from the other side of the door. Little fingers poked under it. I was about to go over and tickle those little fingers. But there was something I needed to do first. I thanked God for giving me these moments to remind me why I do this. For the joy. For the love. For each and every one of my six children.

Now if He could only get them to stop bringing me opossums on a shovel.

Labor of Love

I looked on child-rearing not only as a work of love and duty but as a profession that was fully as interesting and challenging as any honorable profession in the world and one that demanded the best that I could bring it.

ROSE KENNEDY

Little Camper on the Prairie

BY SUE CATRON

O ur family, all ten of us, walking the same streets writer Laura Ingalls Wilder did when she was a girl in Walnut Grove, Minnesota.... I'd pictured this scene in my head for months, and now fifty days into our summer road trip, we were doing just that.

We went inside an early settler's house and saw the long dresses and high-button shoes girls wore back then. What a contrast to my ten-year-old daughter Liza, who was decked out in the red shorts and dirty purple tank top she'd insisted on that morning. "Laura was about your age when she lived here," I said. "Can you imagine wearing a dress like that in this weather?"

Liza jerked away from me. "This is so boring," she said. "This whole trip is boring. Isn't there anything fun to do?"

That wasn't how I'd pictured the scene playing out. I had imagined our family feeling a sense of closeness and togetherness, like the Ingalls family in our favorite TV show, *Little House on the Prairie.*

No, more than imagined. I'd prayed every night since we set out from our house in Iowa on this quest to see the Ingalls family's homesteads that I would finally connect with Liza. My husband, Bill, and I had adopted her out of foster care, like all our kids except our oldest. But unlike our other children, Liza still held back from me, as if she didn't trust my love or that she was really part of our family.

If we do something she's passionate about, I thought, maybe that will make the difference. And Liza loved everything about Laura Ingalls. They were a lot alike—headstrong, smart (sometimes too smart for her own good), constantly getting into trouble, yet somehow irresistible. I looked for books and DVDs to stimulate Liza's quick mind. I brushed her thick, wavy hair every night before bed, hoping that little ritual would grow into a deeper bond. I wanted so badly to give Liza a hug and get just the slightest squeeze back, to feel like mother and daughter. But it seemed like the harder I worked to reach her, the more she pulled away.

From the settlers' home we headed for a one-room red schoolhouse, like the one Laura taught in when she was fifteen. Liza dragged her feet, kicking up huge clouds of dust.

"Liza, please walk correctly," I said.

"Why? I like walking like this."

I took her aside and let the others go ahead with Bill. "You're the main reason we came here," I hissed. "You love watching *Little House*. You're always pretending you're Laura. This is where she really lived. Don't you think that's interesting?"

She shrugged. "Whatever. It's just a bunch of old stuff."

I was so frustrated I felt like kicking the dirt myself. Why had I let Bill talk me into this? Over the years, he's had a lot of cockeyed ideas. But this one took the prize. What if a couple and their eight children—seven of them with special needs—spent 11 weeks together in a 31-foot camper? It sounded like some wacky reality show. Well, my reality was packing lunches, supervising homework, updating the big calendar where I kept track of everyone's activities. I refused to even look at campers with him, but Bill kept at me. "C'mon, we all need a change of scenery," he'd coaxed. "It'll be a blast." And finally—after coming up with the *Little House* angle—I caved in, like always.

That's why we loaded a 31-foot camper with eight scooters, ten bicycles, ten canvas camping chairs, and crates and crates of food, and headed out on the open road. So far we'd visited Burr Oak, Iowa, and Spring Valley, Minnesota, and I kept reminding myself of a line Laura Ingalls Wilder wrote: "Be cheerful in the face of adversity." Then again, she'd never met Liza.

Liza came into our lives at age four, our first foster child. With her big brown eyes and wavy brown hair, she looked more like me than our oldest, Becca, our miracle child, born after years of failed fertility treatments and miscarriages.

It was really for Becca that I'd agreed to be a foster mom. Practically from the moment she could talk, she had asked for a little brother. Even though it hurt to admit it—especially since I knew Bill had dreamed of a big family—I explained to her that we weren't able to have another child.

Then one day Becca came home from school and announced, "I know where we can get me a brother." She handed us a pamphlet with photos of children who needed foster parents.

Bill saw those pictures and his whole face lit up. I knew what that meant. Another one of his wild ideas. "These kids are looking for a good home, and we've prayed for our family to grow," he said. "Maybe this is God's way of answering two needs at once."

I wasn't totally convinced, but I agreed to have Liza and her baby brother move in. We were Liza's third foster family in less than a year. The state classified her as "hard to place." Born to drug addicts, she had a lot of emotional and behavioral issues. She wouldn't let anyone close to her. She smashed toys minutes after we gave them to her. She challenged us on the most basic household rules. And she'd scream hysterically for no reason.

Still, something about Liza tugged at me. A child who tried so hard to push people away...she must have been deeply hurt before. And she had to be aching for love just as deeply. *God, you know I have plenty of love to give,* I said. *Help me be the mom Liza needs.*

Eventually, we adopted Liza and her brother, then five more children, making them a permanent part of our family. If only Liza felt that way! I thought now, watching her march off to the Walnut Grove schoolhouse, kicking up dust all the way. For six years I'd been hoping for a breakthrough. I wondered if it was ever going to come, or if she would always be a stranger in our house.

The sun was beating down when we left the little red schoolhouse. The kids were hungry and irritable. How did the Ingallses survive without air-conditioning? Time for a picnic at Plum Creek, the same creek Laura wrote about some seventy years ago. There was a playground with plenty of space to run. They could burn off some energy while I made sandwiches.

Bill had another idea. "Hey, want to cool off like the Ingalls family? Let's jump in the water!" Within seconds all eight kids were splashing in the creek—in the clothes I had carefully picked out for each of them that morning, except for Liza's. Bill whooped and waded in too. Good thing there's one adult in this family, I thought.

Then I noticed Liza. She was laughing and hollering, taking on four of the other kids in a water fight. I hadn't seen her carefree, not cranky, in months. She and Bill started climbing the slippery rocks. Liza reached out her small hand to grab Bill's— trustingly, the way I longed for her to reach for me. So why wasn't I in the water with her, instead of putting twenty slices of turkey on twenty slices of bread?

It bugged me enough I mentioned it to Bill while the kids were napping that afternoon. "Maybe stop working so hard and just let things happen," he said gently. "It's obvious how much you love Liza. Sooner or later she'll see it too."

By evening we were back at Walnut Grove at the outdoor theater for the Wilder Pageant, a drama based on Laura's stories. The Ingalls family rolled onstage in a covered wagon pulled by two huge horses. Liza, who usually has trouble sitting still for five minutes, moved to the edge of her seat and didn't budge for the next two hours.

At one point she leaned over and whispered loudly, "The Ingallses sure do help each other, don't they?"

"They sure do," I said.

"I guess that's what it means to be a family," she murmured, more to herself than to me. I put my arm around her. This time she didn't pull away.

I don't know what exactly captured Liza's imagination, but in the days that followed, I saw a change in her. While the other kids rushed in and out of cabins and churches and schoolhouses, she lingered and asked questions about what life had been like back then.

Our last stop was De Smet, South Dakota. We saw the surveyor's house from *By the Shores of Silver Lake*. "That's the biggest house Laura lived in when she was a kid," I told Liza.

"It doesn't look very big," she said. "I like our house a lot better." Our house. Had she really called it our house?

By the end of summer we'd covered almost 1,000 miles and spent seventy-five nights in the camper. As we crossed back into Iowa, Liza said, "I can't wait to tell my friends about all the fun my family had camping all summer."

Bill glanced at me and smiled. "What did you like best about the trip?"

"Everything!" she said. "Especially the pageant. It made me feel like an Ingalls. Most of all, it made me glad I'm a Catron." I blinked back a tear. Those were the words I'd waited six years to hear.

A few nights after we got home, Liza sidled up to me, a shy smile on her face. "Mom, would you brush my hair?"

"Of course, honey," I replied, trying not to make a big deal of it.

I'd figured our nightly ritual was another one of my failed attempts to bond with Liza. But here she was, asking me to brush her hair, something she'd never done before. She sat in front of me, and I gently pulled the brush through her thick, beautiful waves, thinking about the summer. Bill was right, our road trip was a blast—and Liza and I were growing closer. Maybe she wasn't the only one discovering how to trust. I was learning too, about when to do my work and when to let God do His.

A Matter of Trust

As a mother, my job is to take care of what is possible and trust God with the impossible.

RUTH BELL GRAHAM

One Look of Love

BY DEENA CLARK FARRIS

I stood in the brightly lit hospital lobby holding my baby daughter, Caitlin. Born prematurely, she had spent six torturous weeks in intensive care and was at last being released to go home. I tried to concentrate on the barrage of instructions a nurse was giving me for her care. "You'll do fine," she finally finished, patting me on the shoulder. I wished I could be so confident. I glanced at my two-year-old son, Patrick, crawling between chair legs nearby. *I've done okay with one child*, I tried to reassure myself. *I can handle another one*. But Patrick had always been a healthy baby. Caitlin had already been on the brink of death. At home there would be no machine to sound an alarm if there was an emergency, no nurse standing by to help.

My hands shook as I tried to buckle Caitlin into her infant seat in our van. "Let me," my husband Carl intervened. He looked at me. "Hey, this is a happy day, remember," he said, brushing away a tear that was sliding down my cheek.

At home I settled into the wide oak rocker with her in the nursery Carl and I had painted yellow and decorated with mobiles. *I'm on my own now*, I thought. I took off Caitlin's bonnet and unbuttoned her pink sweater. I had wanted so much to give

Patrick a sibling, but as I traced my finger along the scars on Caitlin's chest and stroked her shaved head, I wondered how I would handle the added responsibility of a child who had already had so many health problems.

I wrapped her in a blanket and held her against my shoulder. "Hello there, Caitlin," I cooed, rocking slowly.

Patrick clambered up on my lap and squinted at his little sister. "What color are her eyes, Mama?" he asked.

With a start I realized I couldn't say for sure. Caitlin had been sedated or asleep most of the time since her birth. I had never really gotten a good look at her eyes. I held her in front of me, but she turned away. "Look at Mama, Caitlin," I cajoled, peering at her pale face. She kept her eyes tightly closed. "We'll know in time," I assured Patrick. Yet I felt a twinge of frustration that after all the time I had waited to hold my daughter, I would have to wait even longer to know one of the most fundamental things about her.

It was in December that the first labor pains brought me to my knees while I was tending our weather-battered rose garden. At the hospital, doctors gave me medication to halt the contractions and ordered complete bed rest until my April due date.

I had spent the long days on the couch staring out the picture windows, monitoring the time between contractions, and thinking of the son who had been stillborn the previous year after similar complications. I breathed a sigh of relief each time I watched the final few pink streaks of sunset fade into the indigo twilight. Another day closer to a full-term, healthy baby.

It was a drizzly March morning when the contractions couldn't be held off any longer. In the delivery room I reached for my husband's hand as the doctor rushed Caitlin away. "Only a few weeks early," a nurse said to me. "She'll be okay." *God, please let her be all right*, I prayed. But she wasn't. Caitlin was flown forty miles to a neonatal intensive care unit in Houston, where doctors gently prepared me for the worst. Day after day I hoped for a miracle. Seeing her limbs flail as she struggled to get free of the tangle of needles and tubes keeping her alive, I had to look away. *God, please help*, I prayed. But I couldn't really believe in His assistance. After all, I had prayed with the same urgency the year before for my son—only to lose him.

Then, suddenly, Caitlin took a turn for the better. Before I knew it, the doctors were bidding good-bye to the child they had dubbed a "miracle girl." Yet, gazing at her fragile body in the comforting dimness of our own nursery, I felt the same anxiety I had felt while she was in my womb—she was once again in my charge. Patrick scrambled off to play and I placed Caitlin in her crib. "Mama's going to look after you," I murmured, but I shivered at the thought of what might lie in store. I wanted to ask God for help, but wasn't He the one who had put me through all this heartache? Did He even care what I was going through?

Every day I carefully spoon-fed Caitlin, only to watch her spit up time after time. Terrified that her breathing would stop during the night, I moved her crib into our bedroom and slept with one hand on her bony shoulder. Often, I woke up and placed my palm against her chest, checking for her heartbeat. *Why has she had to go through so much?* I demanded of God.

"Caitlin, I love you," I said over and over, but she always kept her face turned away, her eyes squeezed shut. Each time she flinched when I touched her, it felt like rejection. Gazing at her one night, I was filled with a loneliness I had never known before.

The more I thought about it, the more my hurt swelled. God had let me down so many times. Like with Dad. After suspending my education to help care for him when he got sick, I had watched him die at age forty-seven. And Dean. My high school friend had been killed in a car accident after rushing to help with a family crisis. I stood at Caitlin's crib long into the night, interrogating God about the sore spots in my memory, the wounds that had never really healed.

During the following days I felt more and more helpless about Caitlin's unresponsiveness. "Patience," Carl reminded me. "She's still not used to the outside world." But I took her to the pediatrician. The doctor examined her and assured me she was aware of her surroundings and that her physical condition was, in fact, improving.

"Caitlin is ignoring you," she said. "It's a phenomenon I've seen in infants who have received long-term care in trauma units. I think they may be refusing to look their caretakers in the face because they associate them with pain."

Could that possibly be true? I would have done anything to protect her from harm, to erase all the hurt she had already experienced. Yet she linked me with suffering!

That night I settled in the rocker with my sleeping baby. Never before had she seemed so far away from me, not even when she was being kept alive by machines and I wasn't allowed to touch her. I looked at her, cradled against my arm, her head turned away from me as usual. I bent over and softly kissed her. I would never want to hurt her, I thought sadly, I only want to comfort her. I caressed her cheek gently with my finger. *Why so much pain, God?*

That time my question bounced back. Caitlin's behavior reminded me of someone—me. Hadn't I been turning away from God, blaming Him for the hurtful things that had happened in my life just as my baby daughter was associating her own pain with me? Could it be God hated the sadness I had suffered just as much as I hated all Caitlin had gone through? Perhaps my resentment had wounded God just as deeply as my daughter's avoidance was hurting me.

New thoughts surfaced. How Caitlin had survived despite all the odds. How I would never have met Carl had I not gone home to care for Dad when he fell ill. I saw each sorrow from a new perspective, saw how I had been guided and helped through the hard times, how—though I had thought I was alone—God had watched over me just as devotedly as I was watching over Caitlin.

"I'm sorry, Father," I whispered. "I know now I can turn to You." I looked down at Caitlin. "Please help me get through to her."

The next day I rolled Caitlin's crib to the nursery. I fastened pictures of family and friends to the crib's rails, surrounding her with loving faces whose gazes she could not avoid. I took her to the garden with me when I watered and fertilized the sickly roses. But she still turned away and scrunched her eyes tight when I touched her.

Caring for her still took all my energy, but I no longer felt so anxious. When I got frustrated, even with simple things like trying to change her diaper or give her a bath, I reached out to God for help. Caitlin began keeping down her food. Her breathing became stronger. Each night I smoothed lotion onto her scars. "These will fade," I promised her. So will the emotional ones, I told myself.

Caitlin continued to grow healthier, but she still would not face me. "Let me see those pretty eyes of yours," I wheedled. Every time she turned away, I whispered, "Caitlin, I love you!" Even if you never look at me, I love you.

One warm morning I stood in the garden, surrounded by rosebushes laden with colorful blooms. Caitlin dawdled on a blanket at my feet. I picked a red rose and, kneeling, brushed the velvety petals lightly across Caitlin's own rosy cheek. "I love you, Caitlin!" I said for the umpteenth time that day.

And then—finally—she looked at me. I caught my breath and gazed into her big eyes. They were green with gold flecks, the color of a sunlit forest. They were the most beautiful sight on earth. In that one look I saw God's love, through both the good and the bad, and I felt the joy He must feel every time one of His children acknowledges that love.

Love of God

*I am convinced that neither death nor life,
neither angels nor demons, neither the present
nor the future, nor any powers, neither height
nor depth, nor anything else in all creation,
will be able to separate us from the love
of God that is in Christ Jesus our Lord.*

Romans 8:38–39 NIV

A Note from the Editors

Guideposts, a nonprofit organization, touches millions of lives every day through products and services that inspire, encourage, and uplift. Our magazines, books, prayer network, and outreach programs help people connect their faith-filled values to their daily lives. To learn more, visit Guideposts.org or GuidepostsFoundation.org.